THIS BOOK BELONGS TO

THE CHANGING SEASONS

Susan Winget's

THE CHANGING SEASONS

By The Vanessa-Ann Collection

Meredith® Press
New York, New York

For Meredith® Press
Vice-President and Editorial Director: Elizabeth P. Rice
Product Development Manager: Patricia Van Note
Editorial Project Manager: Maryanne Bannon
Production Manager: Bill Rose

For The Vanessa-Ann Collection
Owners:
Jo Packham and Terrece Beesley
Staff:
Gloria Zirkel Baur
Trice Boerens
Sandra D. Chapman
Holly Fuller
Susan Jorgensen
Margaret Shields Marti
Barbara Milburn
Lisa Miles
Pamela Randall
Reva Smith Petersen
Florence Stacey
Nancy Whitley

Photographer: Ryne Hazen

The Vanessa-Ann Collection wishes to thank Every Blooming Thing, Salt Lake City, Utah; Mary Gaskill's Trends and Traditions, Ogden, Utah; The Bearlace Cottage, Park City, Utah; and Dale and Becky Tuttle of Orem, Utah. Their trust and cooperation is always greatly appreciated.

ISBN: 0-696-02364-4
First Printing: 1991
Library of Congress Catalog number: 91-62263

Published by Meredith® Press

Distributed by Meredith Corporation, Des Moines, IA

10 9 8 7 6 5 4 3 2 1

Printed in the United States of America

When asked if she is an accomplished artist, Susan Winget hesitates, and in her lilting Southern drawl replies, "Yes, but . . . I'm just this little person from North Carolina who gets her ideas from family and friends." In fact, she can't quite believe the exposure and acceptance her work receives.

From childhood her artistic talents were evident, though she credits her father, a full-time farmer, for giving her gentle nudges in the confidence department as well as challenges to whet her appetite and keep her interested.

A few years after receiving her bachelor of fine arts from the University of North Carolina at Chapel Hill, shyness prevented Susan from showing her portfolio to a company at a show in Boston. Her husband took the initiative, and she has been represented by them ever since.

Throughout her work, Susan Winget draws from the warm, rich, and brilliant colors of nature. She admits she is partial to the blues and reds so often present in her pictures. After all, she paints amid the rustic atmosphere of a small, refurbished farmhouse studio, where the bold earth hues are a glance away. Also evident is a fiery sunset on the horizon through an airy, open window on the North Carolina family farm. These scenes, as well as those of her children at play in fields amongst the farm animals roaming the pastures, often inspire her drawings.

One day the owners of The Vanessa-Ann Collection spotted her work at a show and immediately approached her about transferring some of her designs to cross-stitch for their fourth book in the American Sampler series. She was flattered and flabbergasted. She was especially excited because she cross-stitches herself and couldn't wait to see her art transferred to a new medium.

The warmth of home and heart are evident in each of Susan Winget's pieces. That she is at peace, content and in harmony with the down-to-earth life-style the family farm affords is obvious. We invite you to cross-stitch her charming down-home scenes to warm your homes and the hearts you touch.

Dear Crafter,

Come share the pleasures of designs sure to win your heart. Noted artist Susan Winget's work has been lovingly transformed into cross-stitch to help you bring the charm and beauty into all corners of your home.

All your country favorites are here—from a country welcome sampler featuring folk toys, dolls, and a patchwork cat, to a crisp autumn sampler.

Susan's art is beautifully illustrated in cross-stitch designs that will make wonderful accents for your home, as well as treasured gifts for loved ones.

We at Meredith® Press strive to bring you the very highest quality craft books, with original designs, clear, easy-to-follow charts, patterns, and instructions. Each project is photographed in full color to help provide easy reference and inspiration for each project you stitch.

We hope you enjoy creating the projects from *The Changing Seasons* and that they become cherished keepsakes in the days to come.

Sincerely,

Pat Van Note

Pat Van Note
Product Development
Manager

CONTENTS

the children were nestled
all snug in their beds
while visions of sugarplums
danced in their heads

*In a child's mind,
time is measured
from one Christmas
to another. Little eyes
sparkle with wonder
at the sight of a tree-
top angel or stockings
carefully filled and
hung by the fire—
assurances of the
warmth of home
and hearth.*

Victorian Christmas

Stitched on cream Pastel Linen 28 over 2 threads, the finished design size is 14⅝" x 11¾". The fabric was cut 21" x 18".

FABRICS	DESIGN SIZES
Aida 11	18½" x 15"
Aida 14	14⅝" x 11¾"
Aida 18	11⅜" x 9⅛"
Hardanger 22	9¼" x 7½"

Anchor **DMC (used for sample)**

Step 1: Cross-stitch (2 strands)

Anchor	Symbol	Half stitch	DMC	Color
1	○	◺○		White
386	•		746	Off White
292	−		3078	Golden Yellow-vy. lt.
891	×	◺×	676	Old Gold-lt.
890	●	◺●	729	Old Gold-med.
933	∴	◺∴	3774	Peach Pecan-med.
868	△		3779	Terra Cotta-vy. lt.
347	▲	◺▲	402	Mahogany-vy. lt.
9	I		760	Salmon
10	▽		3712	Salmon-med.
11	∷		3328	Salmon-dk.
13	×		347	Salmon-vy. dk.
74	+		3354	Dusty Rose-vy. lt.
108	I		211	Lavender-lt.
105	○	◺○	209	Lavender-dk.
101	×		327	Antique Violet-vy. dk.
975	•	◺•	3753	Antique Blue-vy. lt.
920	□		932	Antique Blue-lt.
921	∴		931	Antique Blue-med.
922	×		930	Antique Blue-dk.
159	−		3325	Baby Blue-lt.
133	+		796	Royal Blue-dk.
875	•	◺•	503	Blue Green-med.
206	−		955	Nile Green-lt.
213	△		966	Baby Green-med.
214	□		368	Pistachio Green-lt.
215	∴		320	Pistachio Green-med.
216	+		367	Pistachio Green-dk.
268	■		937	Avocado Green-med.
210	○	◺○	562	Jade-med.
212	×	◺×	561	Jade-vy. dk.
887	U		372	Mustard-lt.
363	□		436	Tan
900	△	◺△	648	Beaver Gray-lt.
397	∷		762	Pearl Gray-vy. lt.

Step 2: Backstitch (1 strand)

Anchor	DMC	Color
236	3799	Pewter Gray-vy. dk.

Step 3: French knot (1 strand)

Anchor	DMC	Color
236	3799	Pewter Gray-vy. dk.

Stitch Count: 204 x 165

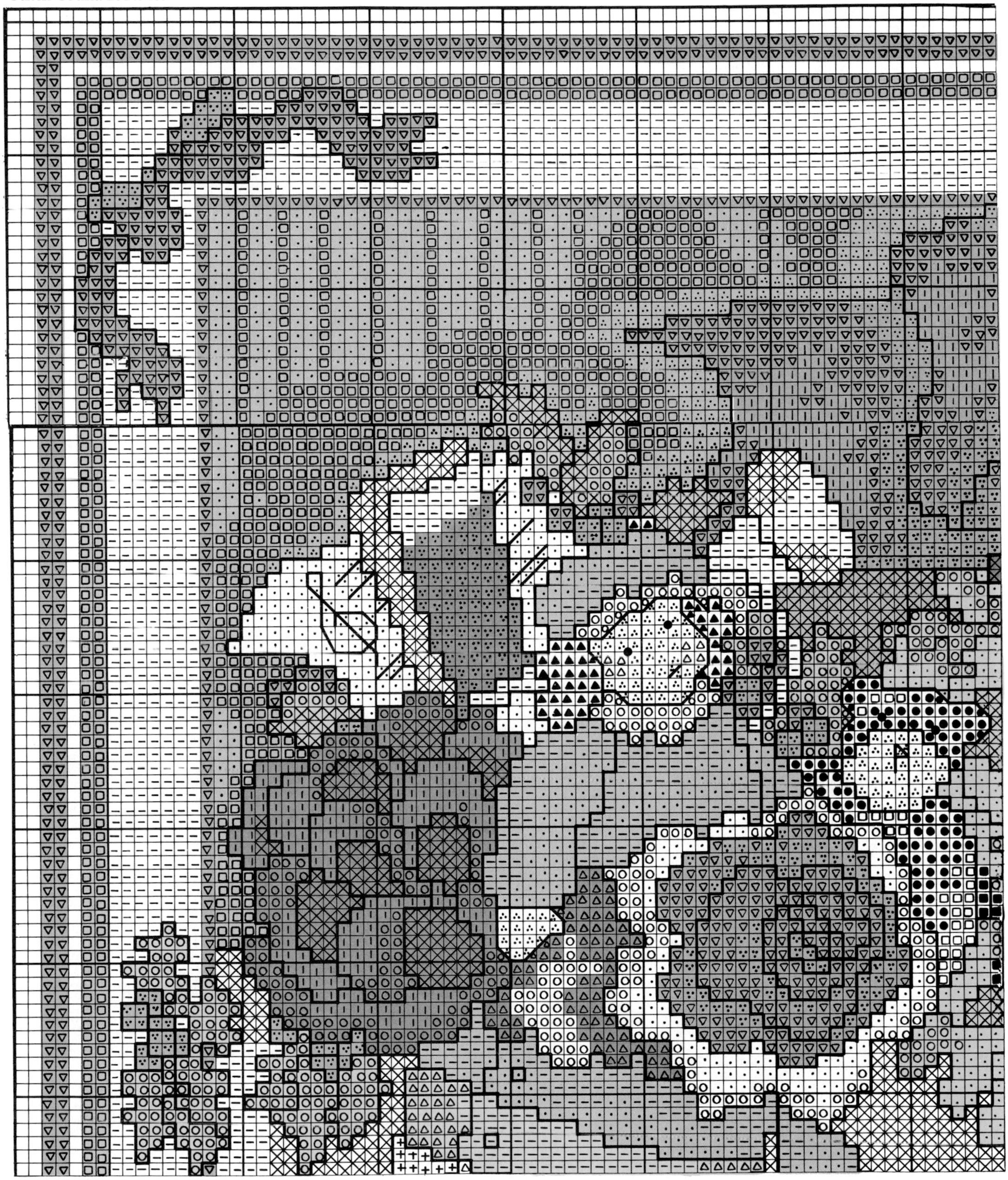

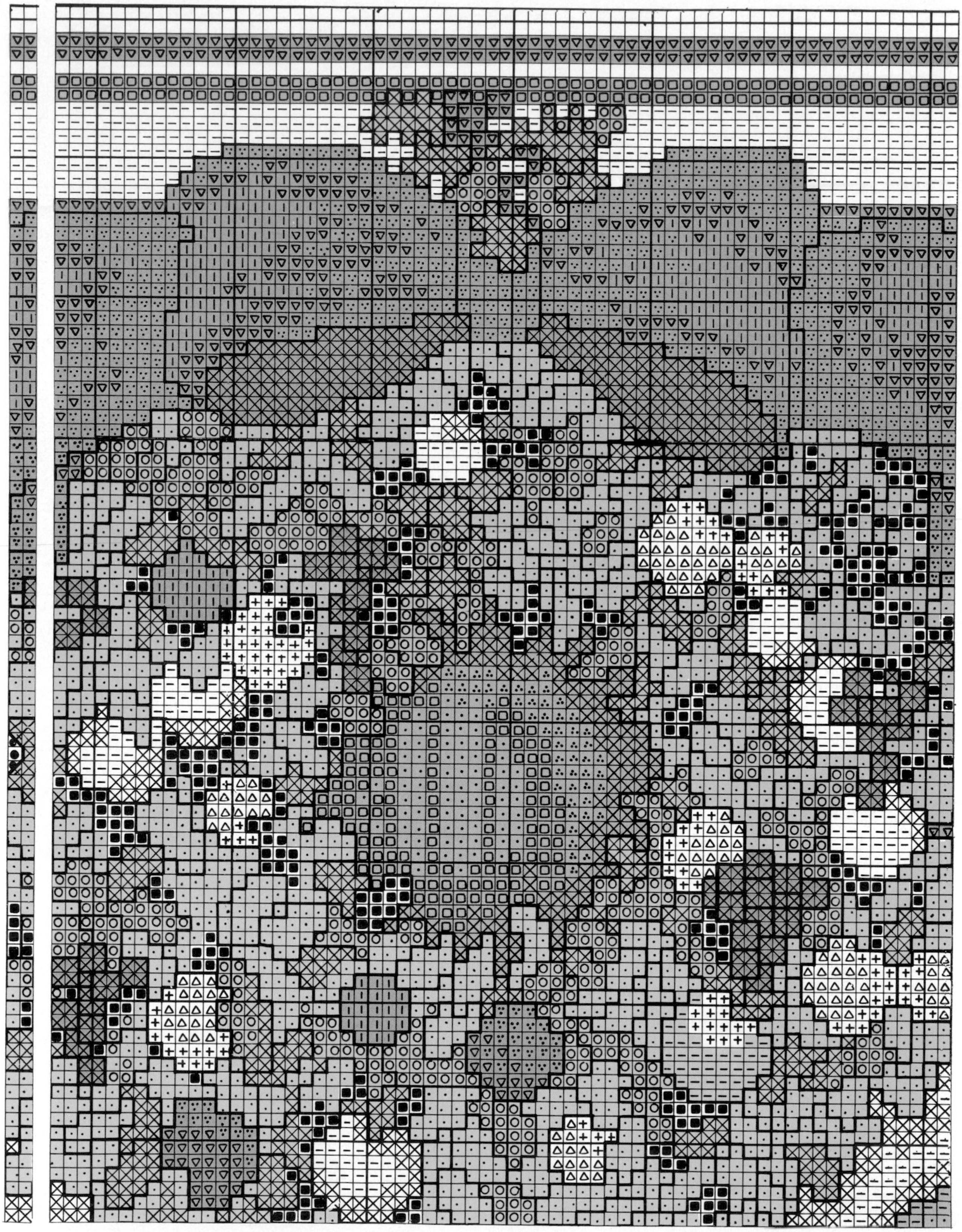

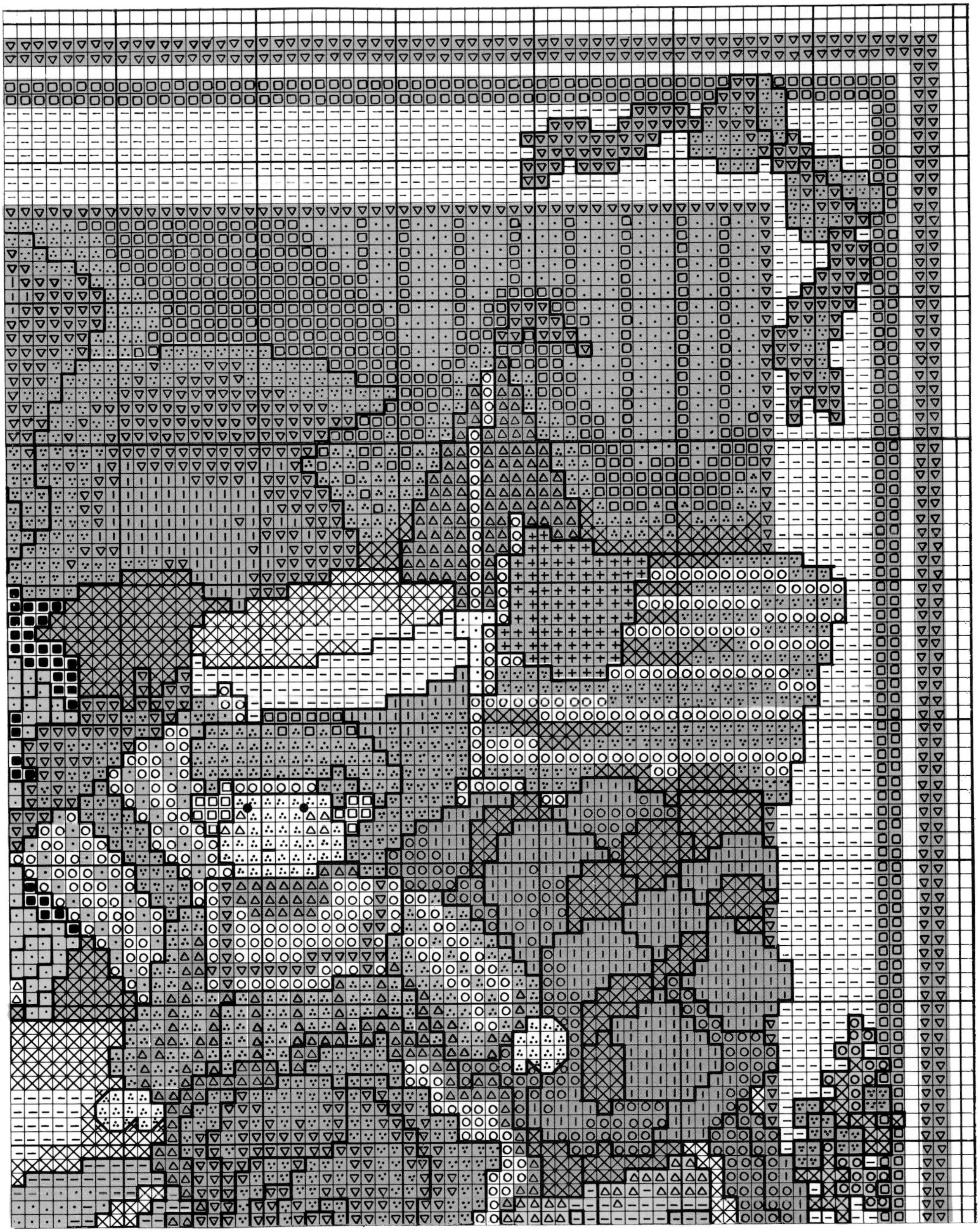

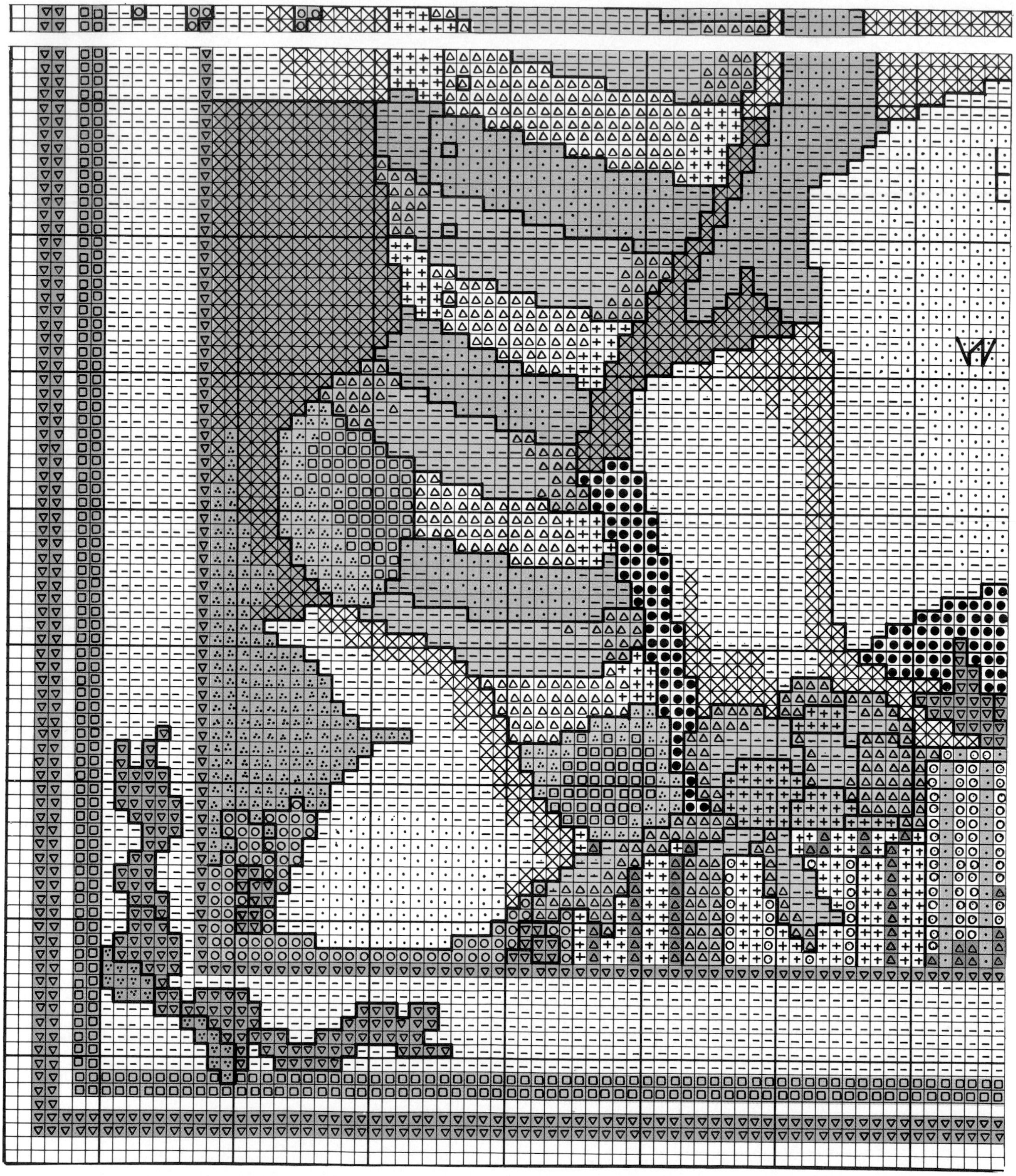

he children were nestled
all snug in their beds
visions of sugarplums
danced in their heads

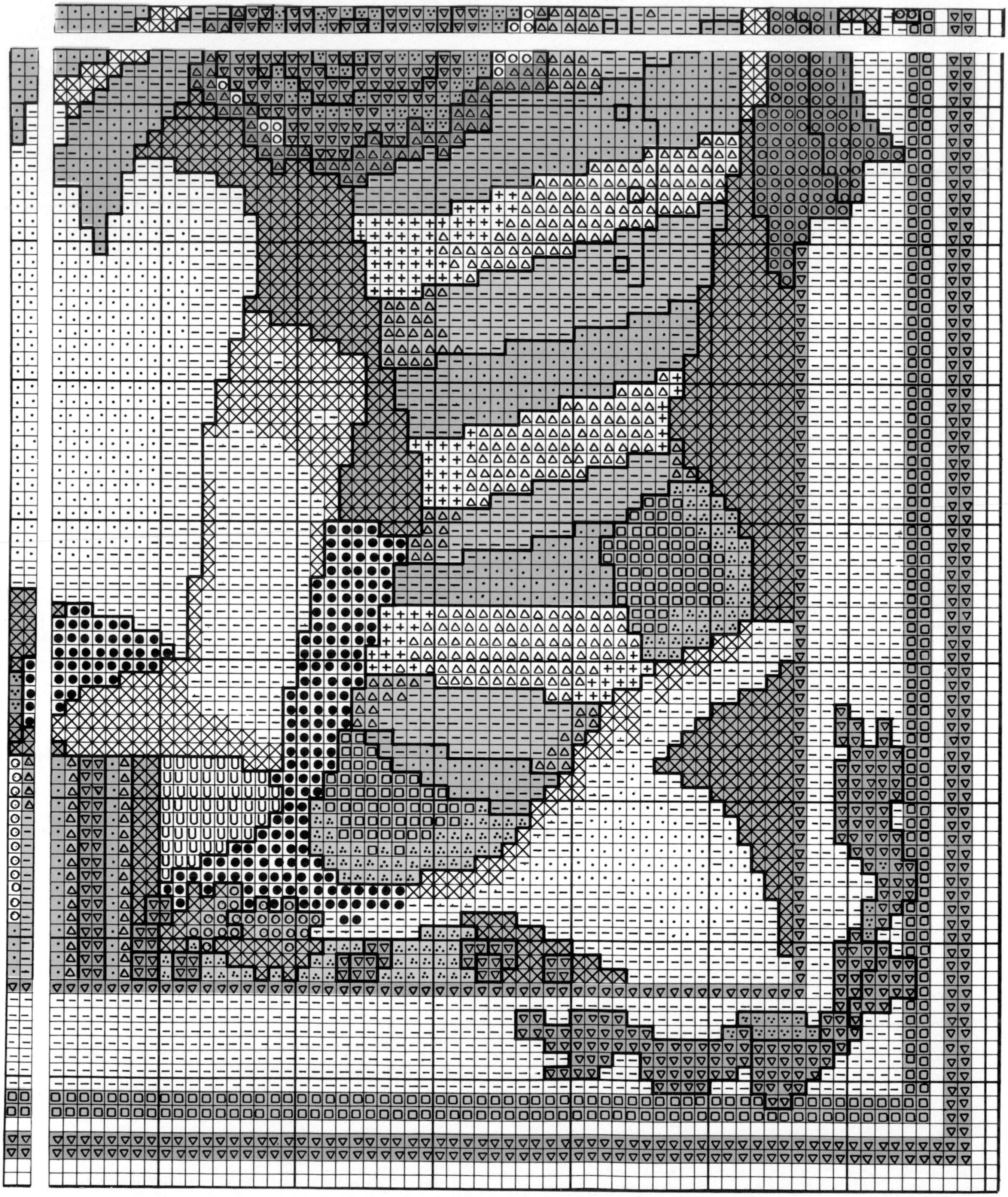

AMY

Pastel Patchwork Stocking

Cat strip: Stitched on pink Dublin Linen 25 over 2 threads, the finished design size for each cat is 1⅜" x 1⅝". Stitch cat five times, ¼" apart. The fabric was cut 9" x 3".

Name strip: Stitched on pink Dublin Linen 25 over 2 threads, the finished design size is not to exceed 7" x 1⅛". The fabric was cut 8¼" x 2⅜". To personalize the stocking, transfer letters to graph paper; begin stitching center letter in center of linen strip.

FABRICS	**DESIGN SIZES**
	Cat Strip
Aida 11	1½" x 1⅞"
Aida 14	1¼" x 1½"
Aida 18	1" x 1⅛"
Hardanger 22	¾" x 1"

Anchor	**DMC (used for sample)**	
	Step 1: Cross-stitch (2 strands)	
896	3722	Shell Pink
875	503	Blue Green-med.
378	841	Beige Brown-lt.
379	840	Beige Brown-med.
	Step 2: Backstitch (1 strand)	
381	838	Beige Brown-vy. dk.
	Step 3: French knot (1 strand)	
381	838	Beige Brown-vy. dk.

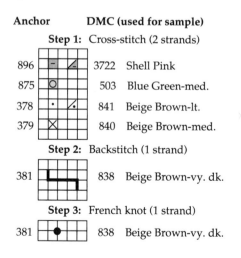

MATERIALS

Two completed cross-stitch designs on pink Dublin Linen 25; matching thread
½ yard of mint green dress-weight linen
½ yard of mint green print
Scrap each of peach and beige dress-weight linen
One 15" x 11" piece of muslin
Scraps of assorted cream laces
½ yard of fleece
Cream thread

DIRECTIONS

1. Trim design pieces to 8¼" x 2¾" for piecing.

2. Cut two stockings from print and two from fleece. Cut one stocking each from mint green linen and muslin. From mint green linen, cut one 3½" x 6½" piece for hanger. From remaining fabrics cut assorted strips 1" to 2½" x 5" to 8½" for piecing. Before piecing stocking front, plan placement of design strips (see photo).

3. To piece stocking front, baste one fleece stocking to wrong side of muslin stocking. Place one print strip over fleece, right side up and matching top raw edges; baste. With right sides facing, place a linen strip over print strip, aligning long straight edge; stitch through all layers (Diagram 1). Turn the linen strip right side up; press (Diagram 2).

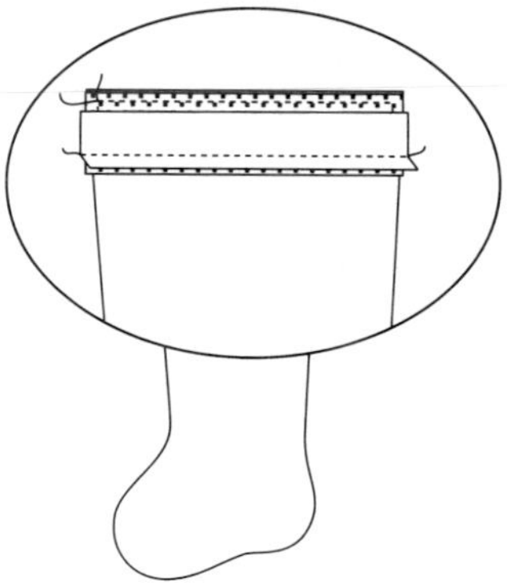

Diagram 1

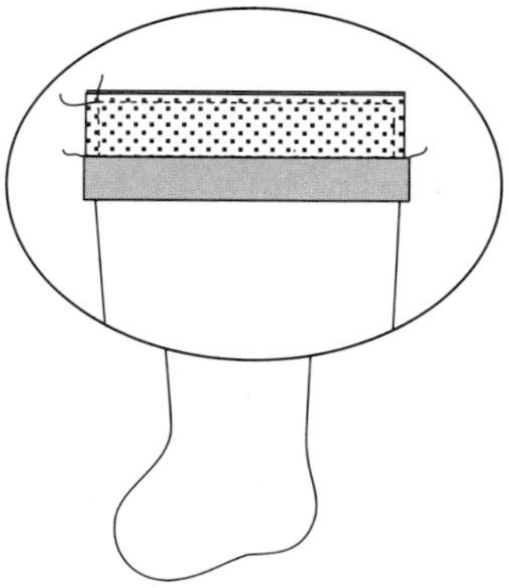

Diagram 2

Repeat process, varying order of strips and incorporating design pieces. Piece strips vertically over toe (see photo) to cover fleece, trimming to match stocking. Attach laces as desired to stocking front (see photo).

4. Baste remaining fleece stocking to wrong side of linen stocking. Stitch stocking front to back with right sides facing, leaving top edge open. Clip curves. Turn.

5. To make hanger, fold hanger with right sides facing to measure 1¾" x 6½"; stitch long edge. Turn. Fold hanger in half with raw edges aligned. Then pin to right side seam of stocking front with raw edges aligned.

6. To make lining, stitch print stockings with right sides facing, leaving top edge open and an opening in seam above the heel for turning. Slide lining over stocking, right sides facing, seams and top edges aligned. Stitch top edge, securing hanger in seam. Turn through opening in lining. Slipstitch opening closed. Fold lining inside stocking.

Cat strip, Stitch Count: 17 x 21

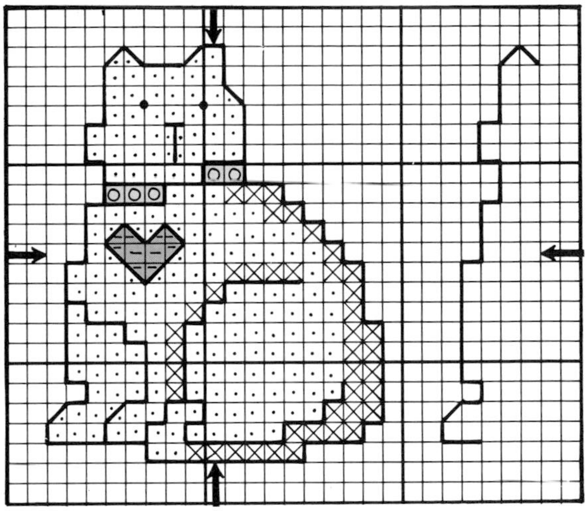

Name strip

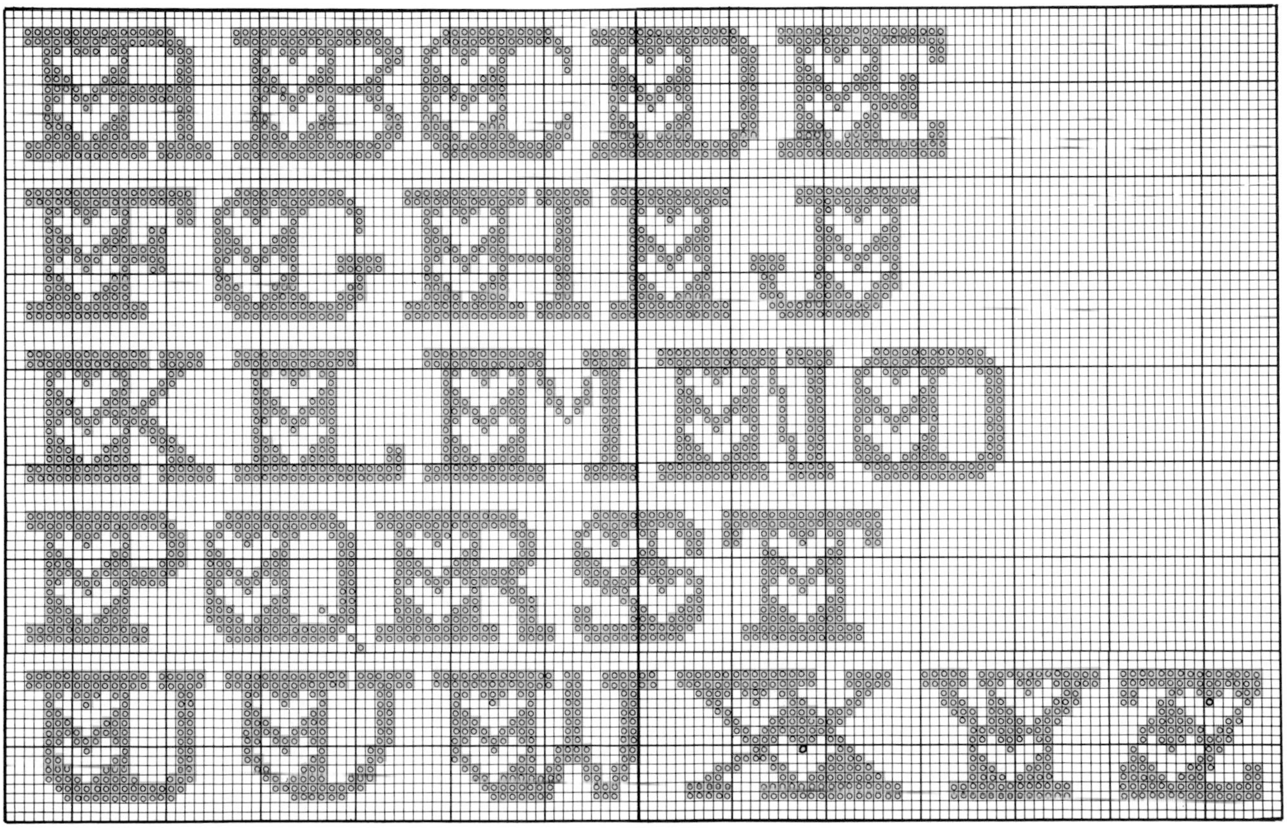

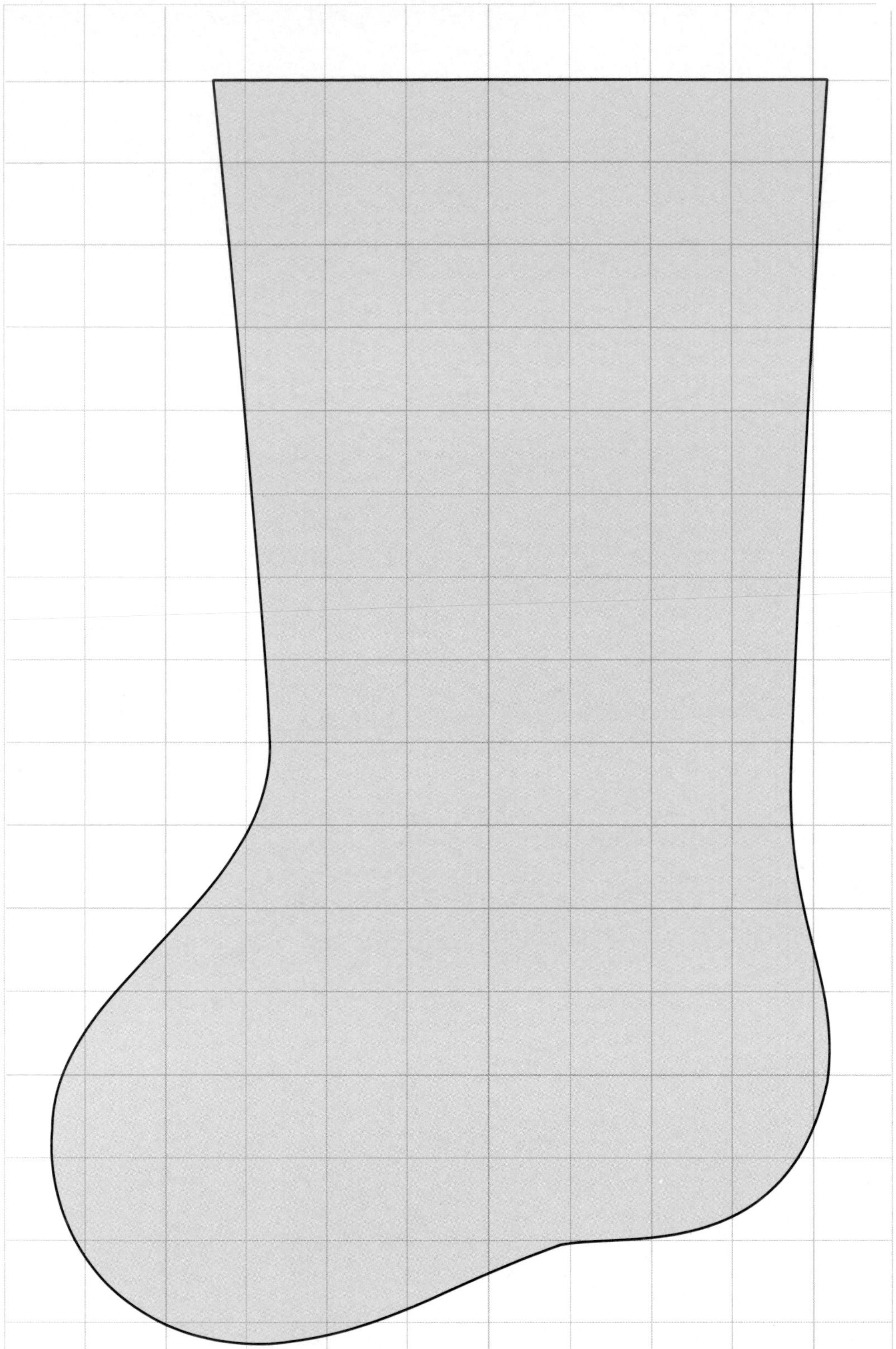

Stocking
1 square = 1"

Little Miss Christmas

Stitched on driftwood Belfast Linen 32 over 2 threads, the finished design size for each tree is 1¾" x 3". Stitch 10 trees, ⅜" apart with bottom row of stitching 4½" from one 25" edge. The fabric (for the dress) was cut 25" x 14".

FABRICS	**DESIGN SIZES**
Aida 11	2⅝" x 4½"
Aida 14	2⅛" x 3½"
Aida 18	1⅝" x 2¾"
Hardanger 22	1⅜" x 2¼"

Anchor	**DMC (used for sample)**	
Step 1: Cross-stitch (2 strands)		
59	326	Rose-vy. dk.
859	3052	Green Gray-med.
862	3362	Pine Green-dk.
379	840	Beige Brown-med.
Step 2: Backstitch (1 strand)		
862	3362	Pine Green-dk.

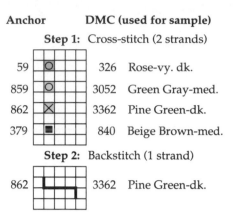

Stitch Count: 29 x 49

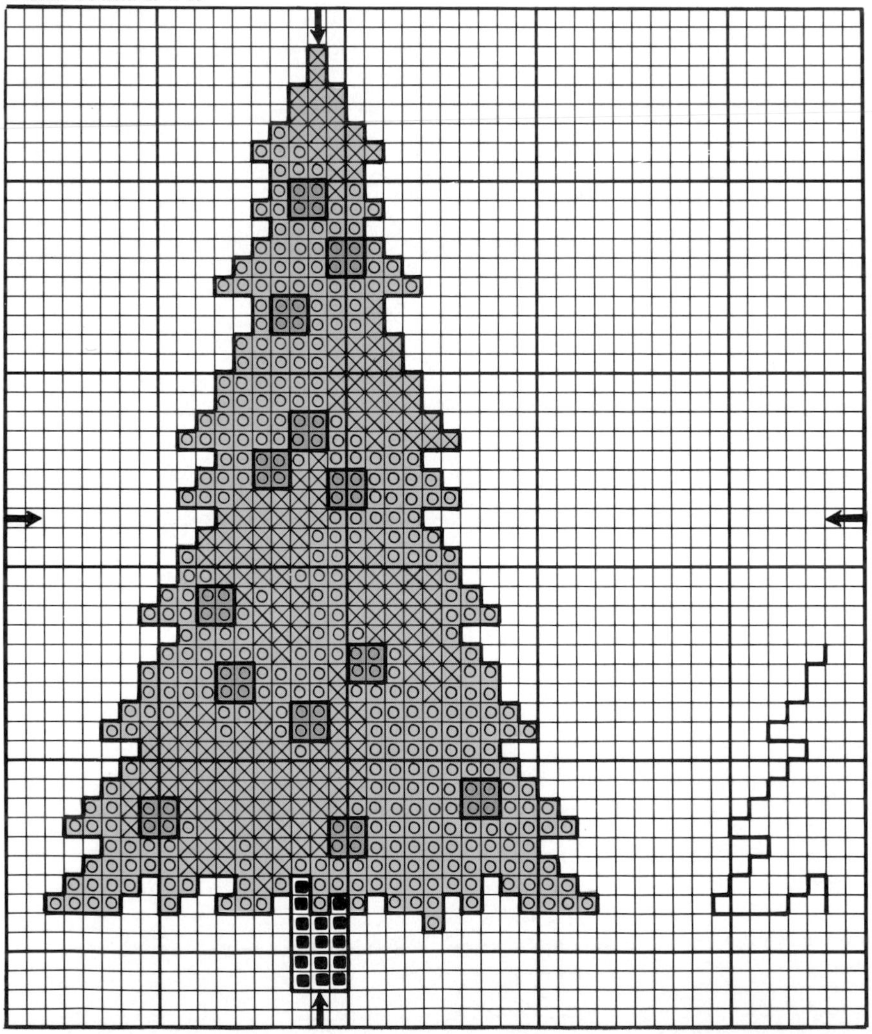

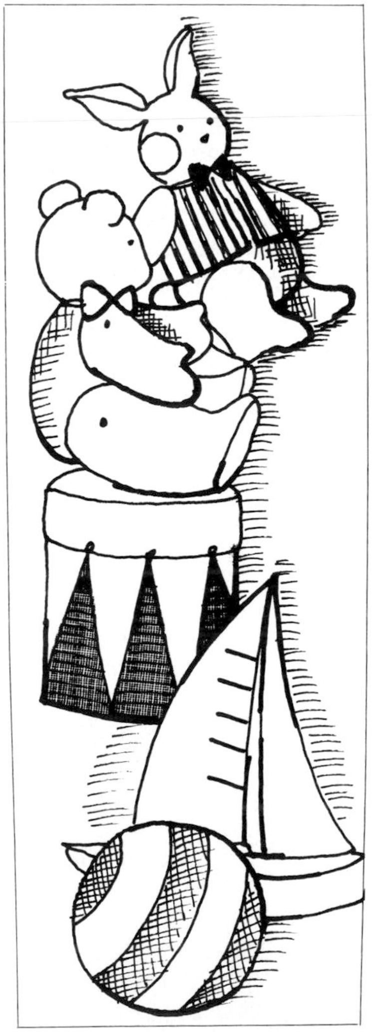

MATERIALS for angel body
One child's white cotton sock (size 6-7½)
8 yards of baby weight white acrylic yarn
Stuffing
Two black tea bags

DIRECTIONS
1. To tea dye sock for an antique look, steep two tea bags in two cups boiling water for five minutes. Remove tea bags; cool to tepid. Add four cups warm water; stir. Soak sock and yarn for 10 minutes in solution, then remove. Place sock and yarn on an old towel; press out excess solution. Let dry on flat surface. The irregular color pattern adds to the antique look.

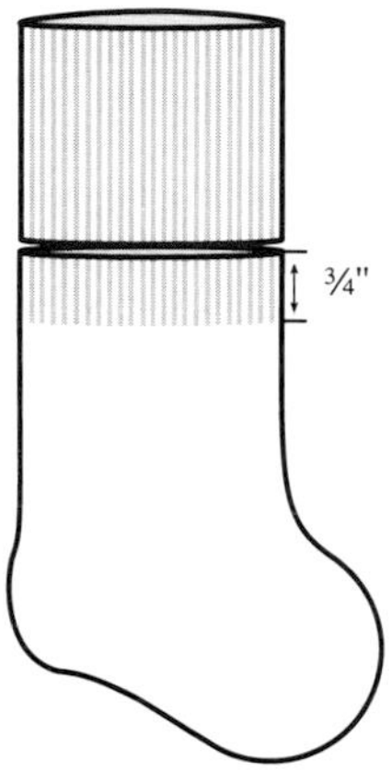

Diagram 1

2. Cut cuff off sock, leaving ¾" of ribbing (Diagram 1). Set sock aside.
To make arms, fold ribbing with right sides facing. Stitch parallel to ribbing, ½" from fold and around one end (Diagram 2). Repeat on other side for other arm. Cut ¼" outside stitching (Diagram 2). Turn each arm. Stuff moderately. Sew running stitches around open ends; pull closed. To form hands, wrap thread tightly ½" from round end of each arm; secure. Set arms aside.

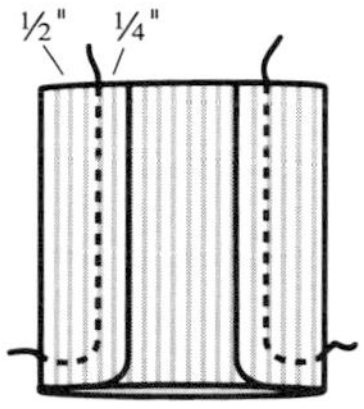

Diagram 2

3. To make legs and body, slit toe of sock. Turn. Beginning with ribbing, stitch legs (Diagram 3), placing "V" at heel of sock (this will be the doll's buttocks). Cut ¼" outside stitching. Turn.

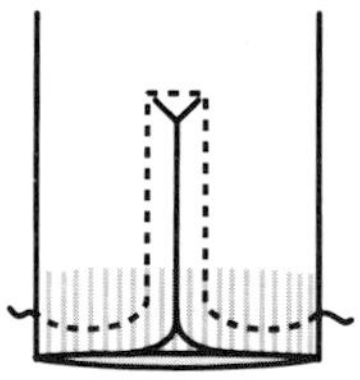
Diagram 3

4. Stuff legs and body moderately. Sew a running stitch around open end; pull closed and secure (this is the top). To form head, wrap thread tightly 1½" from top, shifting stuffing as needed to shape. Whipstitch arms to body just below neck.

5. Make ringlets using yarn (see General Instructions). Fold and tack yarn to head, clipping as desired to make ringlets (see photo).

MATERIALS for dress
Completed cross-stitch design on driftwood Belfast Linen 32; matching thread
One 12½" x 23½" piece of white fabric
¾ yard of 1"-wide white eyelet trim
½ yard of ⅛"-wide cream satin ribbon
¼ yard of 3½"- to 4"-wide lace appliqué for wings (see photo)
One sharp large-eyed needle

DIRECTIONS
1. Tea dye lace appliqué following Step 1 of angel body above. Following pattern in lace, cut two wings. Set aside.

2. Trim design piece to 12½" x 23½", with bottom row of stitching 2" from bottom edge.

3. To make dress, stitch trim ¼" from one long edge on right side of lining. With right sides of lining facing wrong side of design piece, stitch top edges. Open dress/lining to measure 24½" x 23½". Then fold to make an 11¾"-wide tube. Stitch the long edge (this will be the center back seam). Sew a ¼" hem on bottom edge of dress.

4. Fold lining inside dress. Using large-eyed needle and ribbon, make running stitches at ¼" intervals ¼" from neck.

5. To make armholes, stitch two ¾" buttonholes through both layers of dress front (Diagram 4). Cut inside stitching.

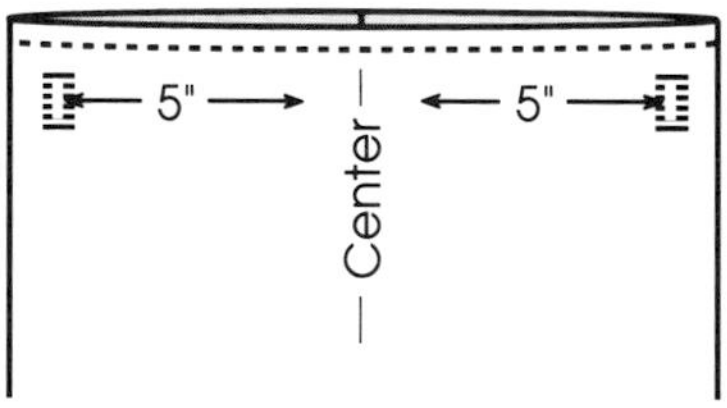

Diagram 4

6. Place dress on angel. Gather ribbon tightly around neck; tie a bow. Tack wings to back of dress.

From the open window, smell the air and feel the breeze that greets a picture-perfect day. Then reach out and invite a friend to share the moment, filled with beauty and love.

Stitch Count: 128 x 104

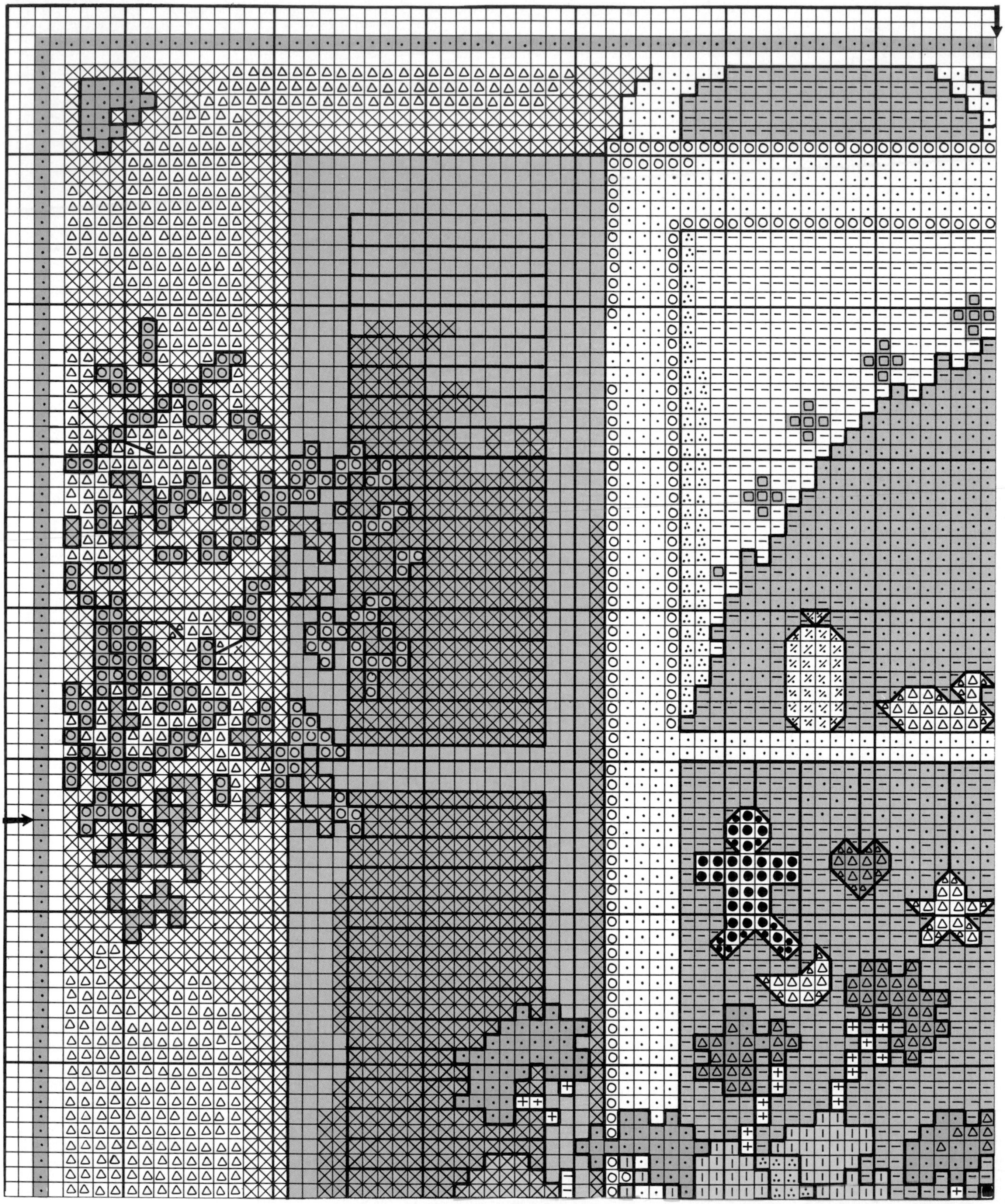

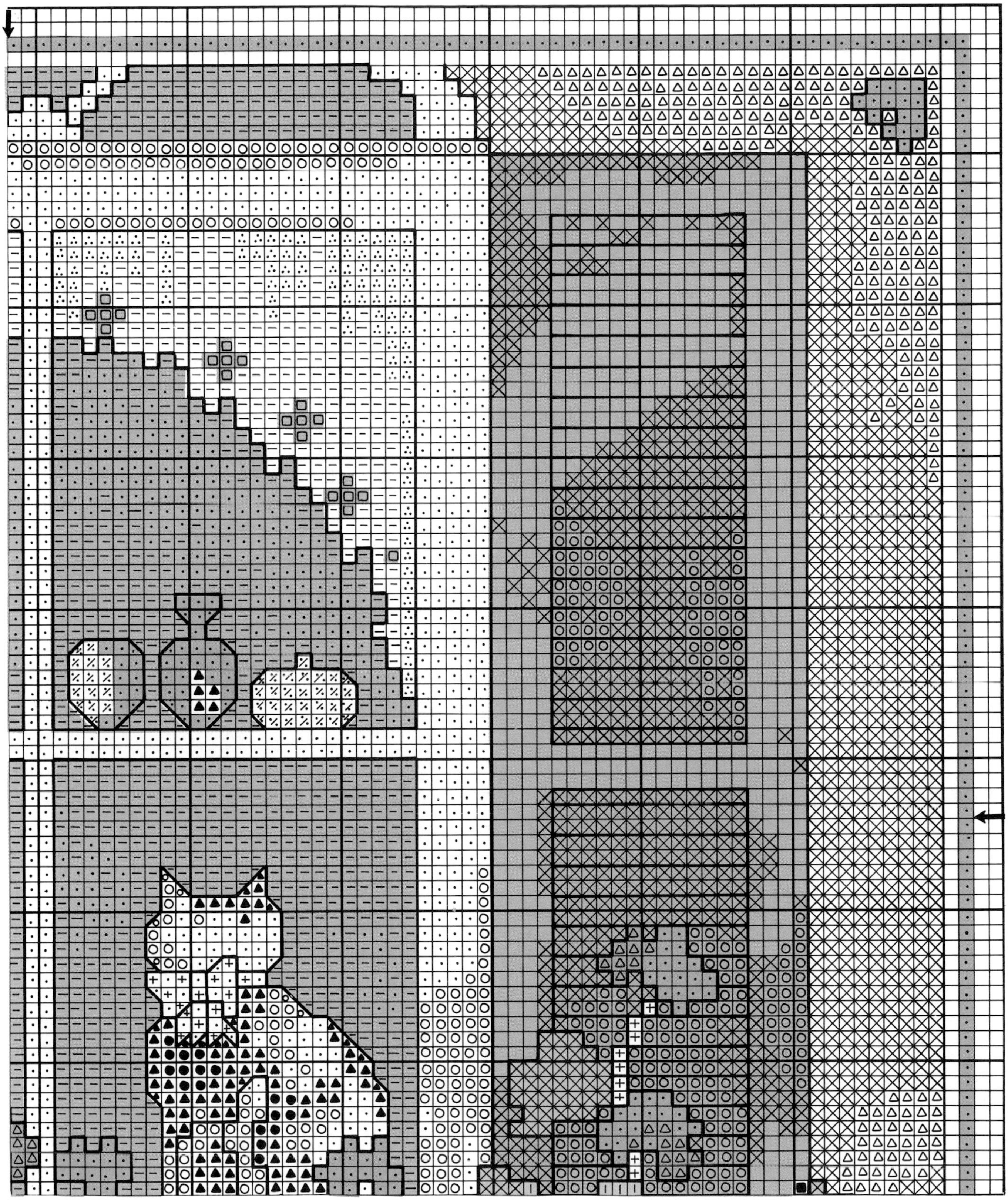

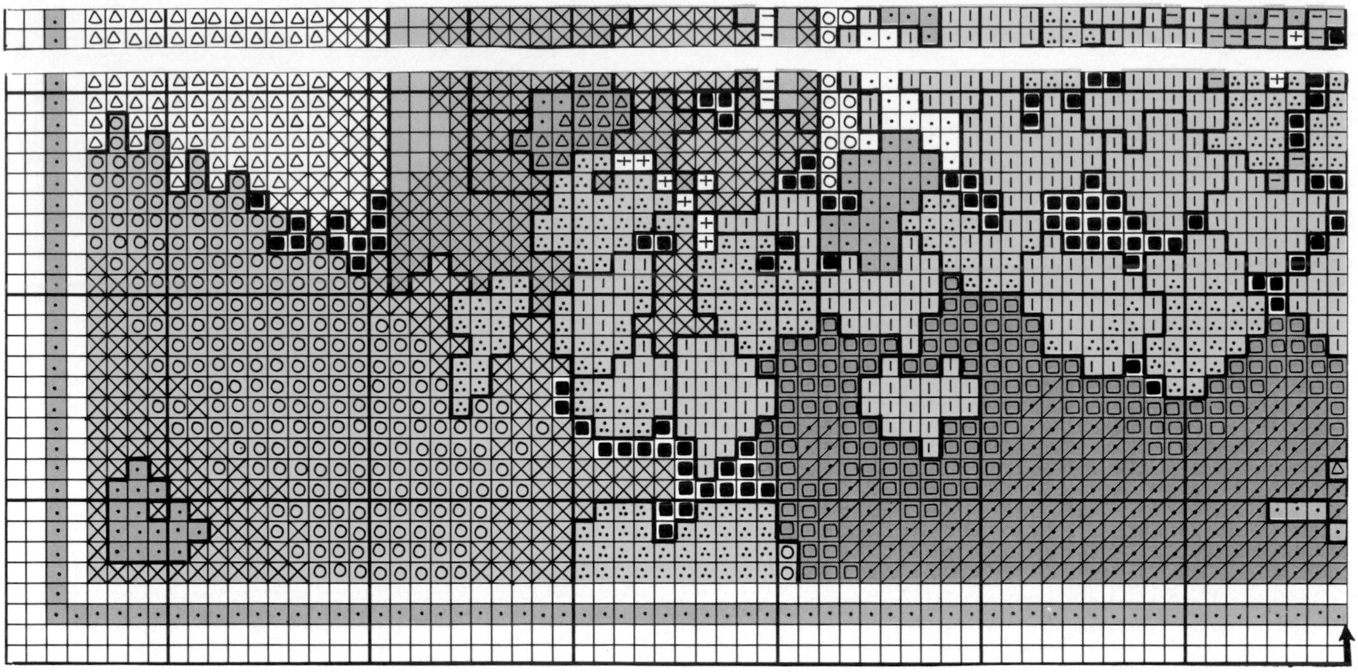

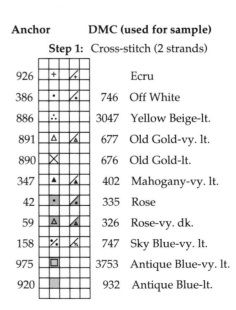

Springtime Window

Stitched on cream Aida 14 over 1 thread, the finished design size is 9⅛" x 7⅜". The fabric was cut 16" x 14".

FABRICS	DESIGN SIZES
Aida 11	11⅝" x 9½"
Aida 18	7⅛" x 5¾"
Hardanger 22	5⅞" x 4¾"

Anchor **DMC (used for sample)**

Step 1: Cross-stitch (2 strands)

Anchor			DMC	
926	+	⁄+		Ecru
386	•	⁄•	746	Off White
886	∴		3047	Yellow Beige-lt.
891	△	⁄△	677	Old Gold-vy. lt.
890	☒		676	Old Gold-lt.
347	▲	⁄▲	402	Mahogany-vy. lt.
42	•	⁄•	335	Rose
59	△	⁄▲	326	Rose-vy. dk.
158	⁒	⁄⁒	747	Sky Blue-vy. lt.
975	▢		3753	Antique Blue-vy. lt.
920			932	Antique Blue-lt.

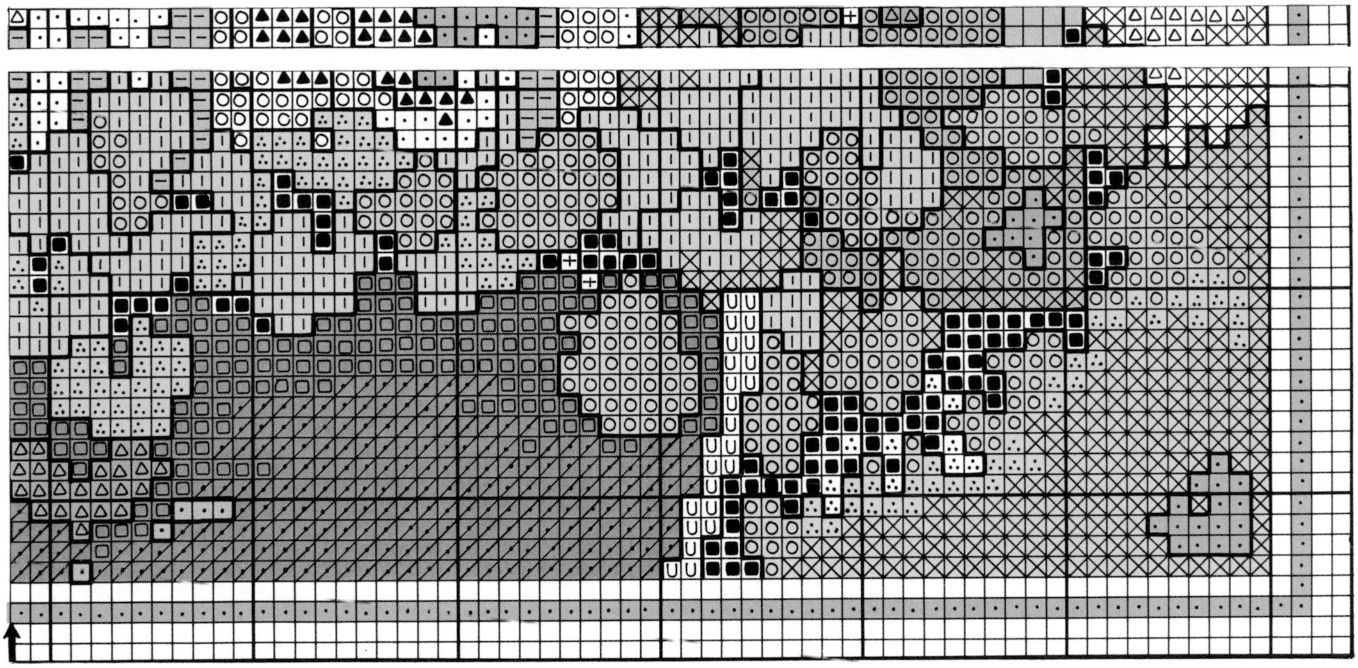

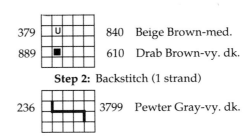

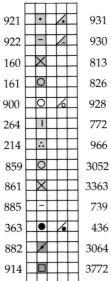

Anchor	DMC	Color
921	931	Antique Blue-med.
922	930	Antique Blue-dk.
160	813	Blue-lt.
161	826	Blue-med.
900	928	Slate Green-lt.
264	772	Pine Green-lt.
214	966	Baby Green-med.
859	3052	Green Gray-med.
861	3363	Pine Green-med.
885	739	Tan-ultra vy. lt.
363	436	Tan
882	3064	Pecan-lt.
914	3772	Pecan-med.
379	840	Beige Brown-med.
889	610	Drab Brown-vy. dk.

Step 2: Backstitch (1 strand)

Anchor	DMC	Color
236	3799	Pewter Gray-vy. dk.

Country Coziness

Tea cozy: The motif is from "Springtime Window." Stitched on pewter Murano 30 over 2 threads, the finished design size is 6⅜" x 6⅜". The stitch count is 95 x 95. The fabric was cut 15" x 10".

Potpourri bag: Stitched on pewter Murano 30 over 2 threads, the finished design size for each watermelon is 1⅝" x ¾". Stitch seven watermelons, ¼" apart. The fabric was cut 9" x 11".

Egg cozy: Stitched on pewter Murano 30 over 2 threads, the finished design size is 2⅛" x 2¼". The fabric was cut 6" x 5".

FABRICS	DESIGN SIZES Potpourri Bag	DESIGN SIZES Egg Cozy
Aida 11	2¼" x 1"	2⅞" x 3"
Aida 14	1¾" x ¾"	2¼" x 2⅜"
Aida 18	1⅜" x ⅝"	1¾" x 1⅞"
Hardanger 22	1⅛" x ½"	1⅜" x 1½"

Egg Cozy and Potpourri Bag

Step 1: Cross-stitch (2 strands)

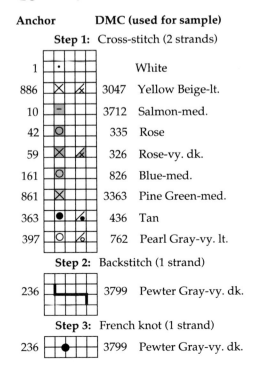

Anchor	DMC (used for sample)	
1		White
886	3047	Yellow Beige-lt.
10	3712	Salmon-med.
42	335	Rose
59	326	Rose-vy. dk.
161	826	Blue-med.
861	3363	Pine Green-med.
363	436	Tan
397	762	Pearl Gray-vy. lt.

Step 2: Backstitch (1 strand)

Anchor	DMC	
236	3799	Pewter Gray-vy. dk.

Step 3: French knot (1 strand)

Anchor	DMC	
236	3799	Pewter Gray-vy. dk.

MATERIALS for tea cozy

Completed cross-stitch design on pewter Murano 30
One 15" x 10" piece of unstitched pewter Murano 30
½ yard of dark blue floral print fabric; matching thread
½ yard of fleece
1 yard of ⅛"-wide piping

DIRECTIONS

1. Place tea cozy pattern over design piece with design centered horizontally and with bottom edge 2¾" below design; cut. Cut one tea cozy from unstitched Murano, two from print fabric and two from fleece. From print fabric, cut 1"-wide bias strips, piecing as needed to equal 29". Make 29" of corded piping.

2. To make cozy, stitch corded piping on curved edge of design piece with right sides facing and raw edges aligned. Baste one fleece cozy to wrong side of each Murano cozy. Stitch Murano cozies with right sides facing, sewing on stitching line of piping and leaving straight edge open. Clip curves. Trim fleece from seam allowance; turn.

3. To make lining, stitch curved edge of print cozies with right sides facing and raw edges aligned, leaving straight edge open and an opening in curved edge for turning. Slide lining over cozy, right sides facing and raw edges aligned; stitch straight edge. Turn. Slipstitch opening closed. Fold lining inside cozy.

MATERIALS for potpourri bag

Completed cross-stitch design on pewter Murano 30
One 7" x 10" piece of unstitched pewter Murano 30
½ yard of dark blue floral print fabric; matching thread
Two 7" x 10" pieces of muslin
¾ yard of ⅛"-wide cording
1 yard of ⅜"-wide pink picot ribbon
2 cups of potpourri (see General Instructions)

DIRECTIONS

1. With design centered vertically and bottom row of stitching 1¼" from short edge, trim design piece to measure 7" x 10". Cut one 14" x 14" piece from print fabric and 1"-wide bias strips, piecing as needed to equal 27". Make 27" of corded piping.

2. To make bag, baste one muslin piece to wrong side of each Murano piece. Then stitch corded piping, right sides facing and raw edges aligned, on two long edges and one short edge. Stitch Murano pieces with right sides facing and raw edges aligned, leaving short edge with no corded piping open. Clip corners; turn.

3. To make lining, fold 14" x 14" print piece with right sides facing and raw edges aligned to measure 7" x 14"; stitch the long edge and one short edge, leaving an opening for turning in long seam. Slide lining over bag, right sides facing, raw edges and seams aligned; stitch the top edge. Turn. Slipstitch opening closed. Fold lining inside bag with the top edge 2" above seam to form casing and ruffle. Topstitch on seam through all layers. Also topstitch ½" above and parallel to seam. Carefully clip side seam threads in casing. Thread ribbon through casing. Insert potpourri. Pull ribbon tightly; tie in a bow.

MATERIALS for egg cozy
Completed cross-stitch design on pewter Murano 30
One 5" x 4" piece of unstitched pewter Murano 30
Scrap of dark blue floral print fabric; matching thread
Scrap of fleece
12" of ⅛"-wide cording

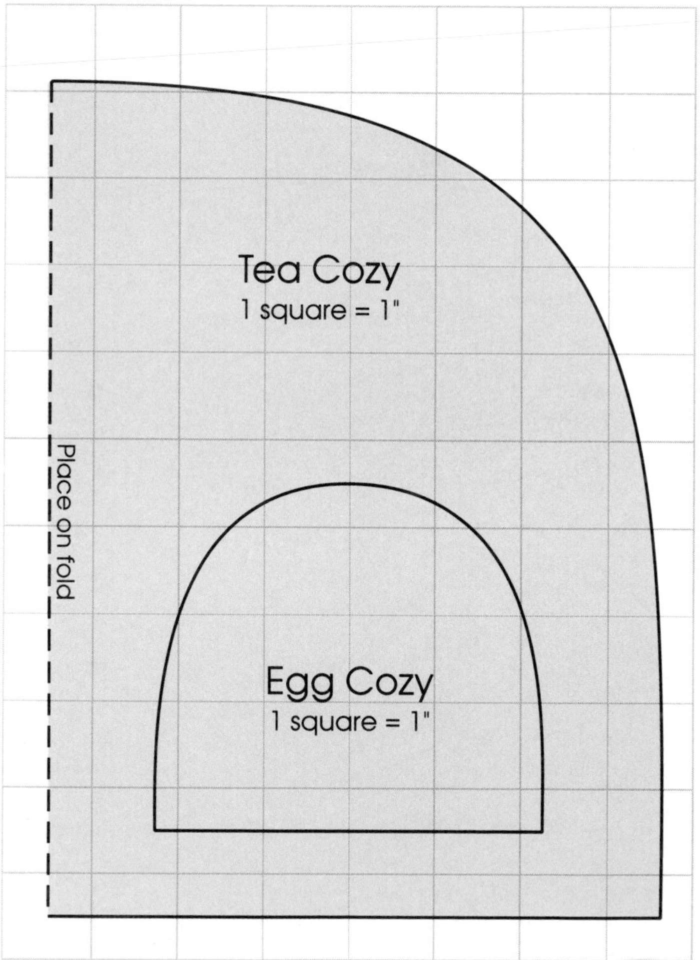

DIRECTIONS
1. Place egg cozy pattern over design piece with design centered horizontally and with bottom edge 1" below design; cut. Cut one egg cozy from unstitched Murano, two from print fabric and two from fleece. Cut 1"-wide bias strips, piecing as needed to equal 12". Make 12" of corded piping. Make egg cozy following Steps 2 and 3 of tea cozy.

Potpourri Bag, Stitch Count: 25 x 11

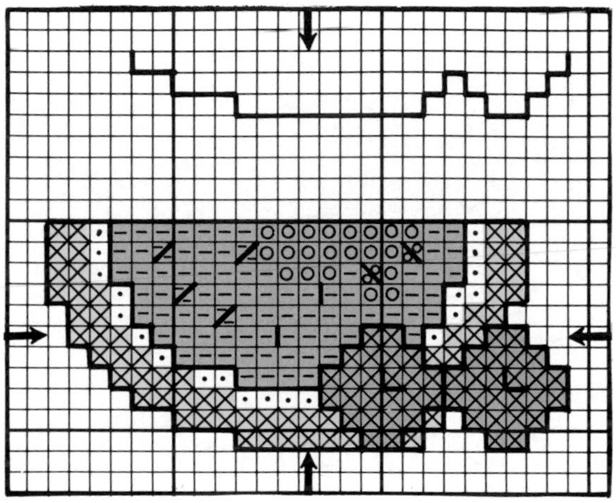

Egg Cozy, Stitch Count: 31 x 33

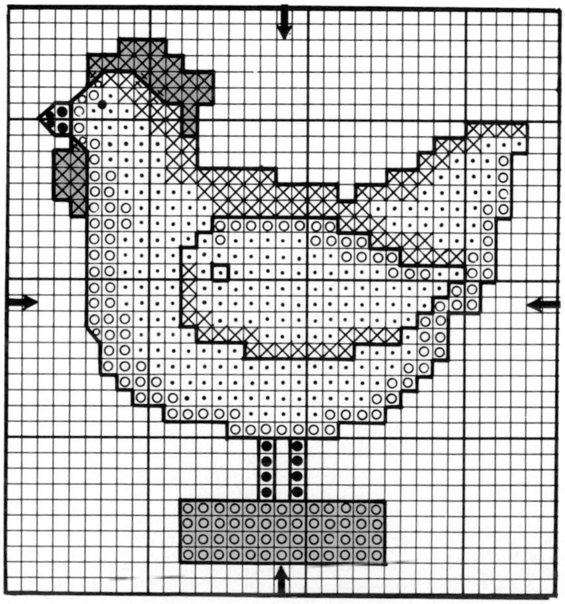

THE BOBBSEY TWINS
AT MEADOW BROOK

A Sewing Treasure Chest

Stitched on beige Hardanger 22 over 1 thread, the finished design size is 2¼" x 3". The fabric was cut 7" x 7".

FABRICS	DESIGN SIZES
Aida 11	4½" x 6⅛"
Aida 14	3½" x 4¾"
Aida 18	2¾" x 3¾"

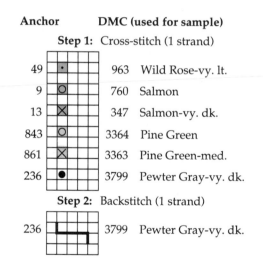

Anchor **DMC (used for sample)**

Step 1: Cross-stitch (1 strand)

Anchor	Symbol	DMC	Color
49	•	963	Wild Rose-vy. lt.
9	O	760	Salmon
13	X	347	Salmon-vy. dk.
843	O	3364	Pine Green
861	X	3363	Pine Green-med.
236	●	3799	Pewter Gray-vy. dk.

Step 2: Backstitch (1 strand)

Anchor	DMC	Color
236	3799	Pewter Gray-vy. dk.

MATERIALS

Completed cross-stitch design on beige Hardanger 22
½ yard of burgundy print fabric; matching thread
¾ yards of ⅞"-wide peach/cream braided trim
1¾ yards of ⅛"-wide salmon satin ribbon
¾ yard of fleece
One 22" x 28" piece of poster board
Scrap of cotton
Glue gun and glue

Note: To make the blue sewing box, substitute the burgundy print fabric with navy blue, the peach/cream braided trim with gold/blue, and the salmon ribbon with light blue.

DIRECTIONS

1. To make bottom of box, cut the following:

   One 6" x 6" piece of fabric
   One 4" x 4" piece of poster board

   Center poster board on wrong side of fabric. Fold edges of fabric over edges of board; glue (Diagram 1). Glue fabric edges of each remaining piece in this fashion.

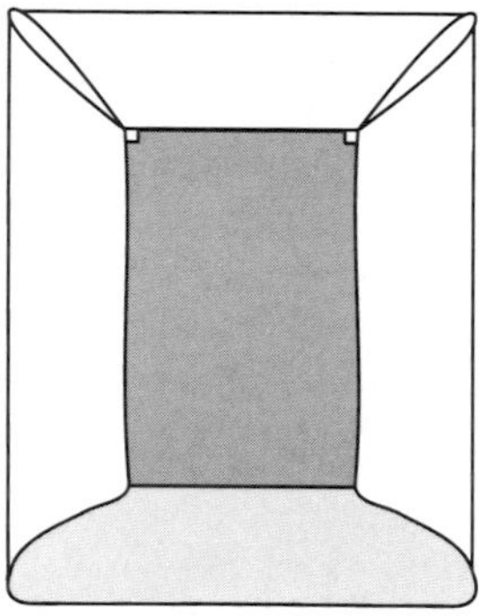

Diagram 1

2. To make large panels, cut the following:

   From poster board:
   One large panel piece
   Four 3½" x 4" pieces for pads
   From fabric:
   One large panel piece, adding 1" to all edges
   Four 5¼" x 5¾" pieces for pads
   From fleece—four pieces in each of the following sizes: 3¼" x 3¾", 3⅛" x 3⅝", 3" x 3½"
   From ribbon: Eight 4½" lengths

   Clip inside corners of fabric panel piece (Diagram 2). Center poster board panel piece on wrong side of fabric. Glue fabric edges to poster board.

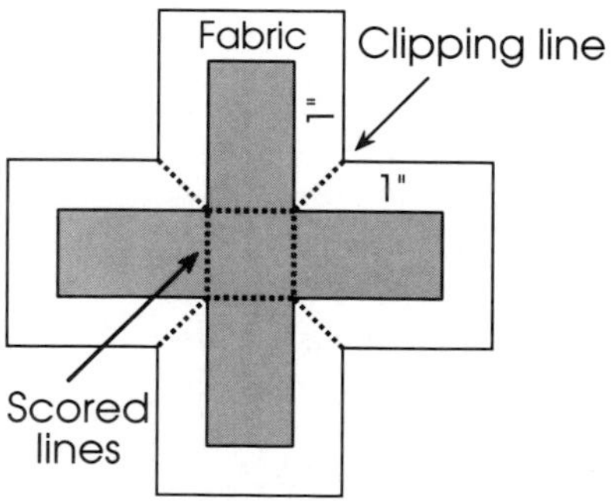

Diagram 2

Layer one poster board pad, three fleece pieces (from large to small), and one fabric pad (right side up). Glue fabric edges to poster board. Place two ribbons horizontally parallel over stuffed side of pad and glue ends to back.

Repeat to make three more pads. Center one pad over each panel; glue. Center large panels over bottom of box with wrong sides facing; glue.

3. To make small panels, cut the following:

From poster board:
One small panel piece
Four 1½" x 2¾" pieces for pads
From fabric:
One small panel piece, adding 1" to all edges
Four 1⅜" x 2⅝" pieces for pads
From fleece: Four 1⅛" x 2⅜" pieces for pads
From ribbon: Four 2½" lengths

Repeat Step 2 using small panel pieces and one piece of ribbon for each panel. Center small panels over bottom of large panels. Rotate 45° (see photo); glue.

4. To make inner box, cut the following:

From poster board:
One inner box piece
One 1" square
From fabric:
Two inner box pieces, adding ¼" to all edges
One 1½" square

Score lines on poster board inner box (see pattern); fold along scored lines. Machine stitch fabric inner boxes, with right sides facing, leaving long edge open. Clip corners. Turn. Insert posterboard inner box. Slipstitch opening closed. Fold on scored lines to form box (see photo); glue side and bottom. Center box over bottom of small panels (see photo); glue.

Cover poster board square with fabric. Stuff cotton inside inner box. Place square, wrong side down, inside inner box.

5. To make hinge, cut one 4½" x 7" piece of fabric. Fold fabric in half, with right sides together, to measure 2¼" x 7". Using ¼" seam allowances, stitch raw edges, leaving one short edge open. Clip corners. Turn. Center long seam in back; press. Set aside.

6. To make box lid, cut the following:

From poster board:
One box lid piece
Two 4⅛" x 4⅛" pieces
From fabric:
One box lid piece, adding 1" to all edges
Two 6⅛" x 6⅛" pieces
From fleece—two pieces in each of the following sizes: 4⅛" x 4⅛", 3⅞" x 3⅞", 3⅝" x 3⅝", 3⅜" x 3⅜"
From braid:
One 16½" length
One 5" length

Trim the design piece to 5½" x 5½", centering design. Layer one 4⅛" x 4⅛" poster board, four fleece pieces (from large to small), and design piece (right side up). Glue design piece edges to poster board. Set aside.

Score lines on poster board lid (see pattern). Fold along scored lines to form lid; glue. Clip inside corners of fabric lid 1". Center poster board lid on wrong side of fabric lid. Fold edges of fabric to inside of board; glue. Center under design piece, with flat sides facing; glue. Glue 16½" braid to sides of lid (see photo).

Glue finished short end of hinge to outside of one large panel, 2½" below top edge and centered horizontally. Glue opposite end of hinge to inside of lid so that large panels fit snugly inside lid. Fold remaining braid in half. Glue ends inside lip of lid at front, centered horizontally (see photo).

Layer remaining poster board, fleece pieces (from large to small) and fabric (right side up). Glue fabric edges to poaster board. Glue flat side to inside of lid.

Stitch Count: 50 x 67

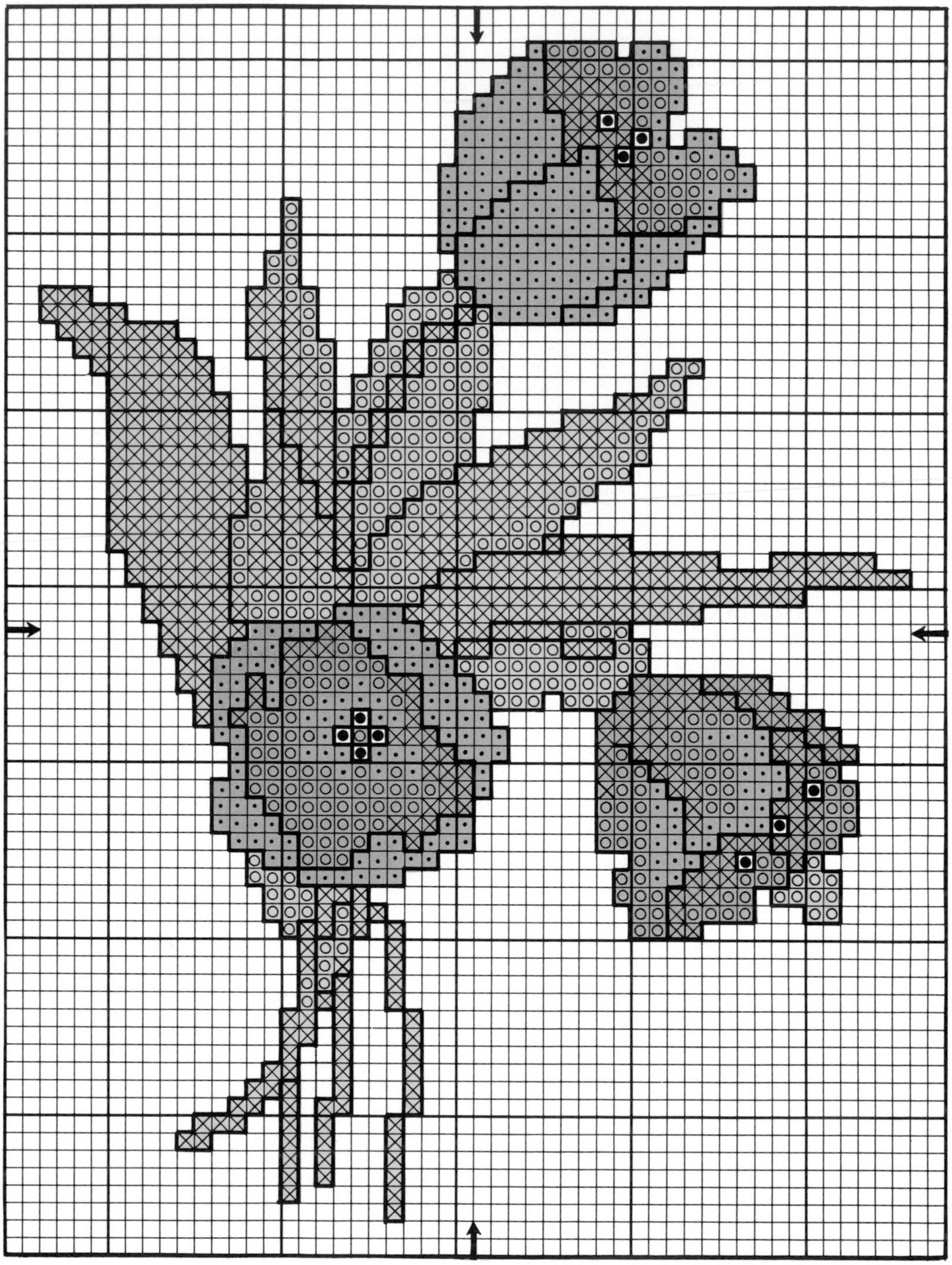

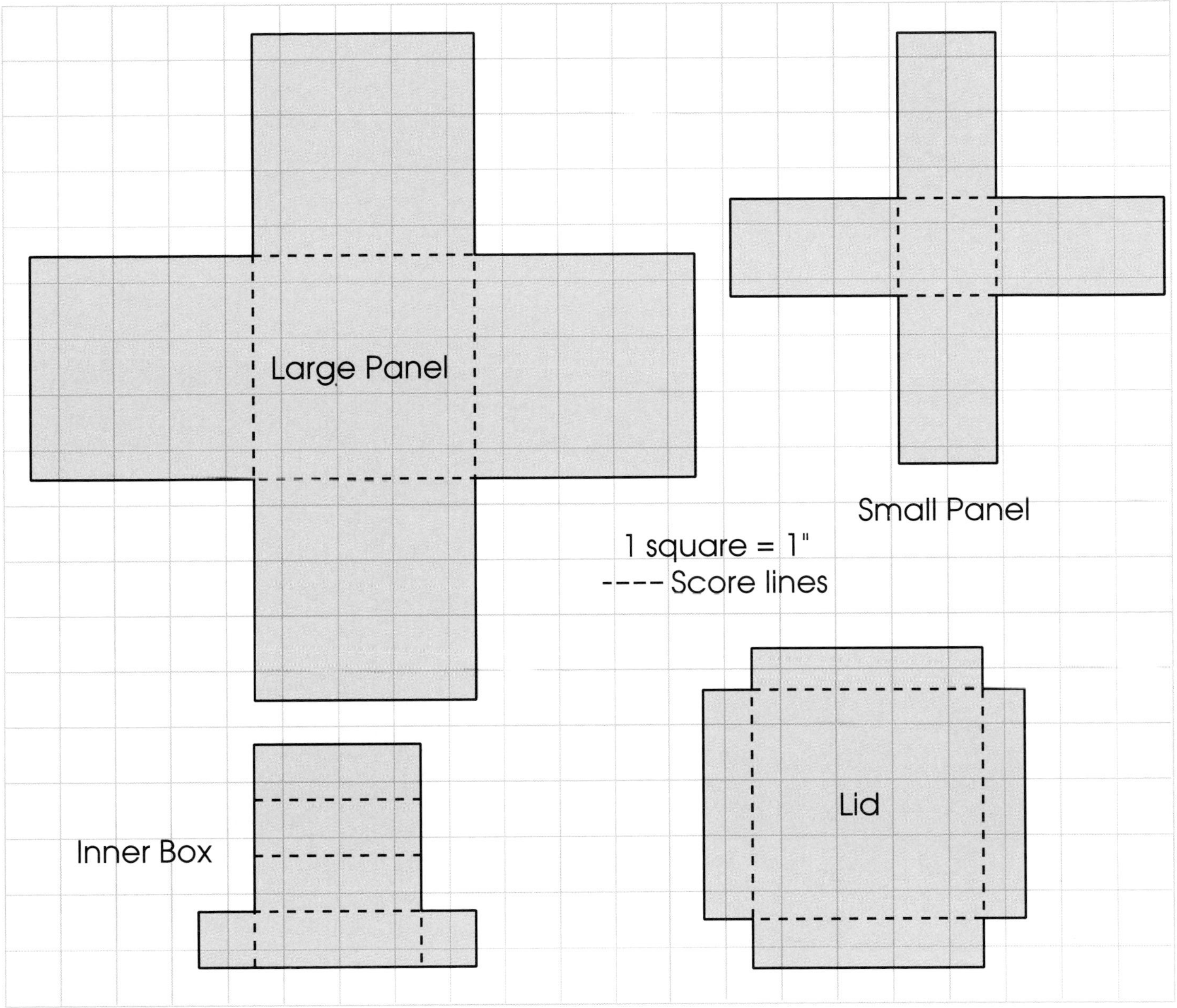
Large Panel
Small Panel
1 square = 1"
---- Score lines
Inner Box
Lid

Sitting on the front porch with time to dream need not be a fantasy. Join the artist in this scene—she has saved a comfortable chair just for you, and asks only that you not disturb the cat!

XXX

Country Welcome

Stitched on cream Damask Aida 14 over 1 thread, the finished design size is 12⅛" x 9⅞". The fabric was cut 19" x 16".

FABRICS	**DESIGN SIZES**
Aida 11	15½" x 12½"
Aida 18	9½" x 7⅝"
Hardanger 22	7¾" x 6¼"

Step 1: Cross-stitch (2 strands)

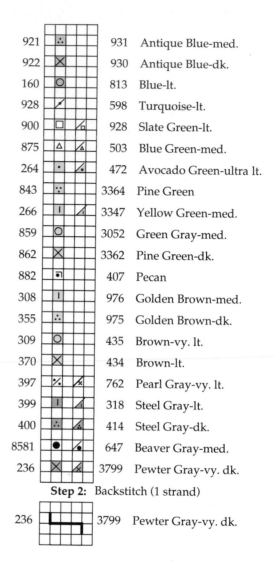

Anchor	DMC (used for sample)	
1		White
288	445	Lemon-lt.
886	677	Old Gold-vy. lt.
890	729	Old Gold-med.
893	224	Shell Pink-lt.
894	223	Shell Pink-med.
74	3354	Dusty Rose-vy. lt.
42	309	Rose-deep
108	211	Lavender-lt.
118	340	Blue Violet-med.
343	3752	Antique Blue-ultra vy. lt.
921	931	Antique Blue-med.
922	930	Antique Blue-dk.
160	813	Blue-lt.
928	598	Turquoise-lt.
900	928	Slate Green-lt.
875	503	Blue Green-med.
264	472	Avocado Green-ultra lt.
843	3364	Pine Green
266	3347	Yellow Green-med.
859	3052	Green Gray-med.
862	3362	Pine Green-dk.
882	407	Pecan
308	976	Golden Brown-med.
355	975	Golden Brown-dk.
309	435	Brown-vy. lt.
370	434	Brown-lt.
397	762	Pearl Gray-vy. lt.
399	318	Steel Gray-lt.
400	414	Steel Gray-dk.
8581	647	Beaver Gray-med.
236	3799	Pewter Gray-vy. dk.

Step 2: Backstitch (1 strand)

Anchor	DMC	
236	3799	Pewter Gray-vy. dk.

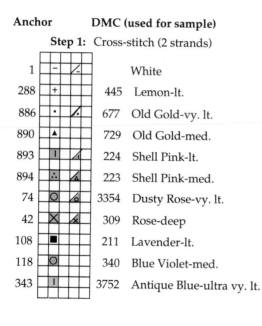

Stitch Count: 170 x 138

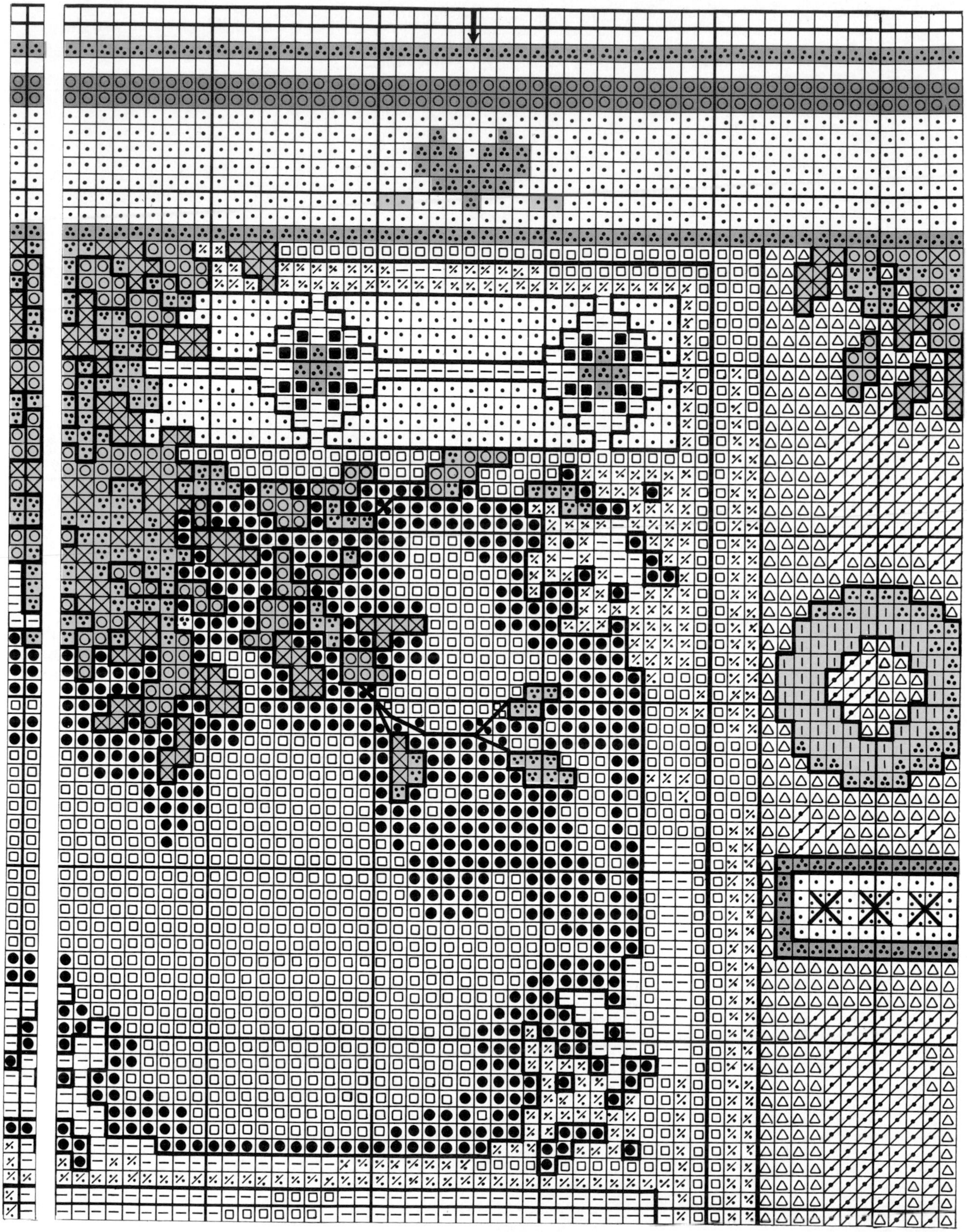

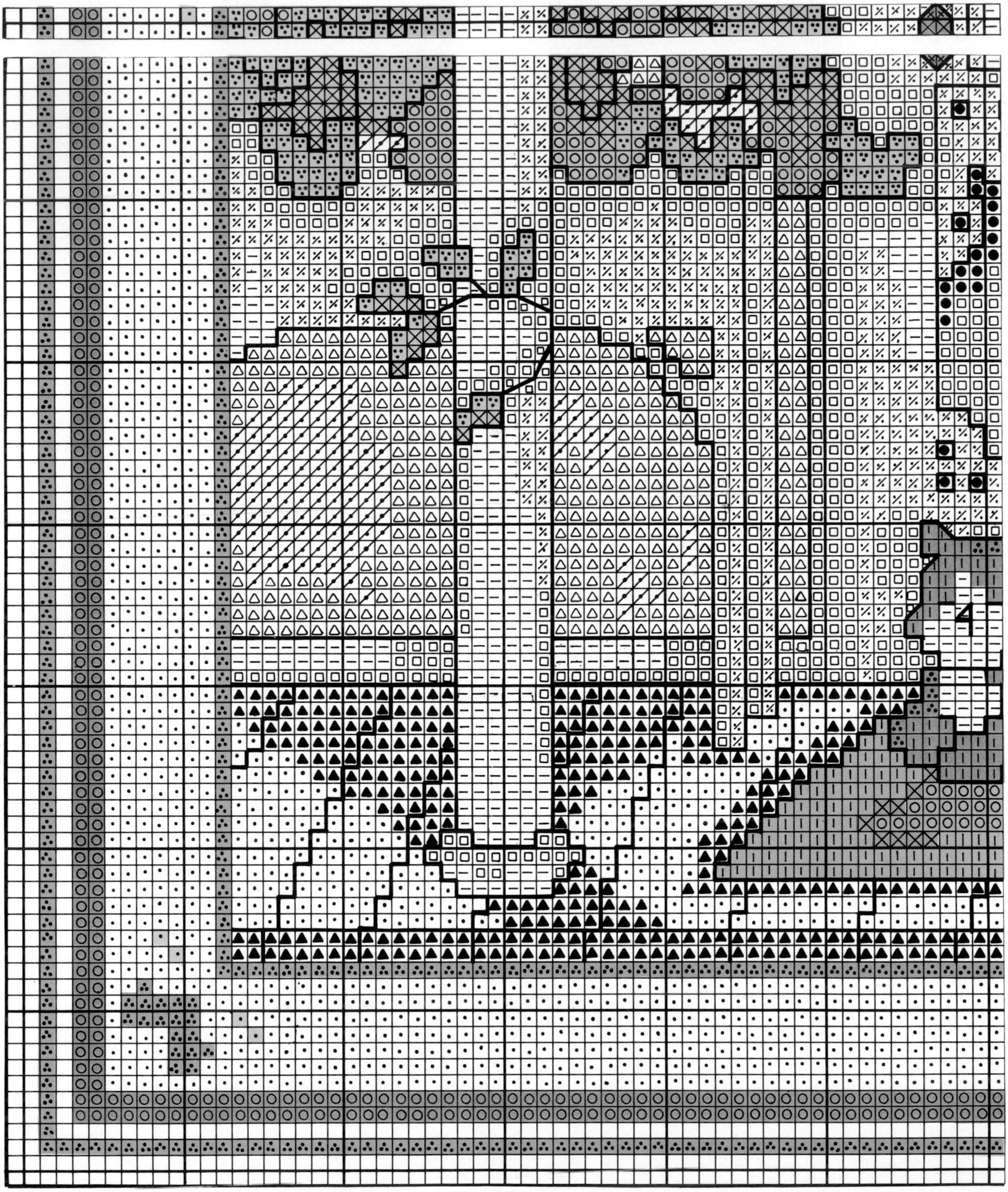

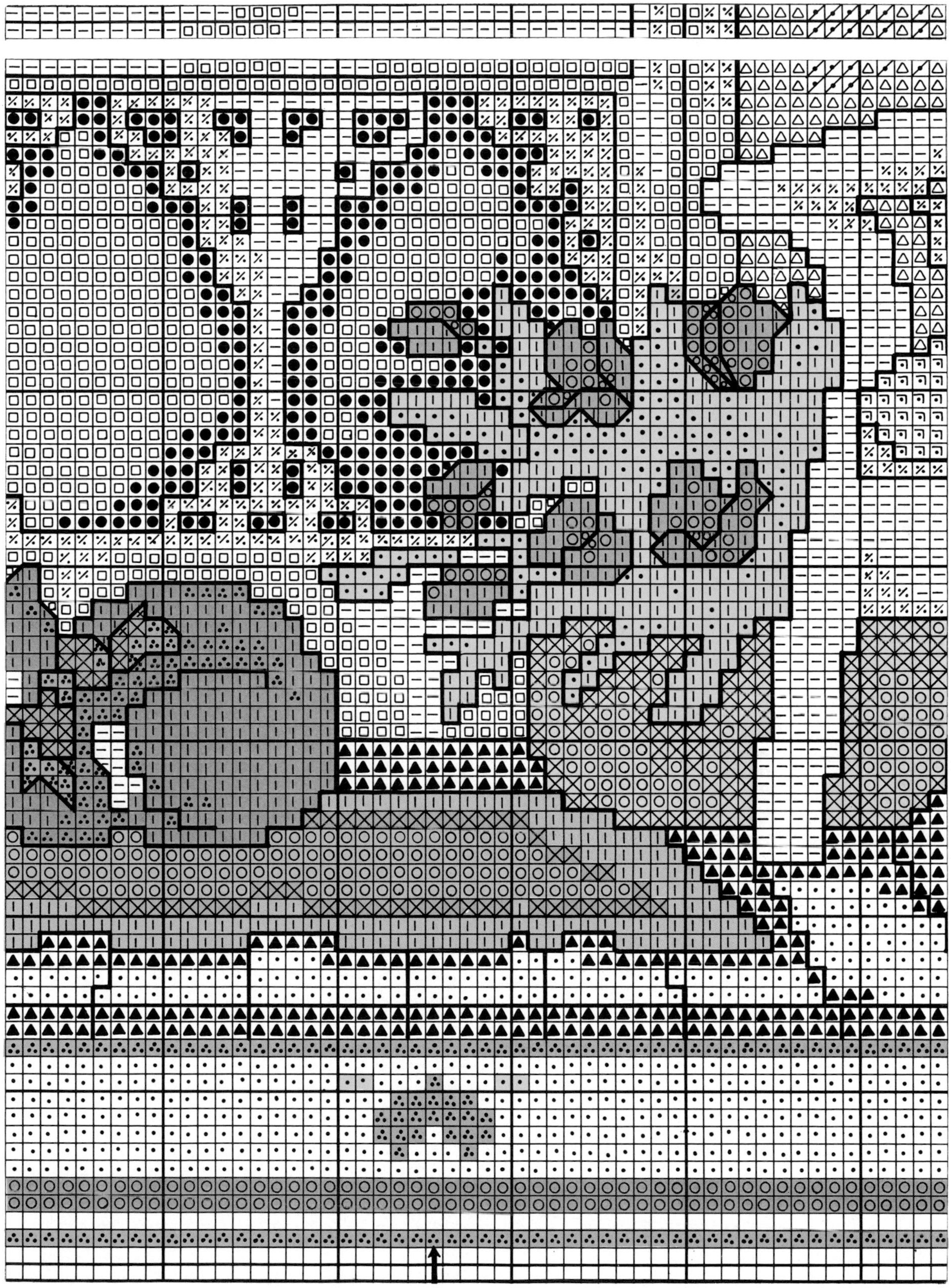

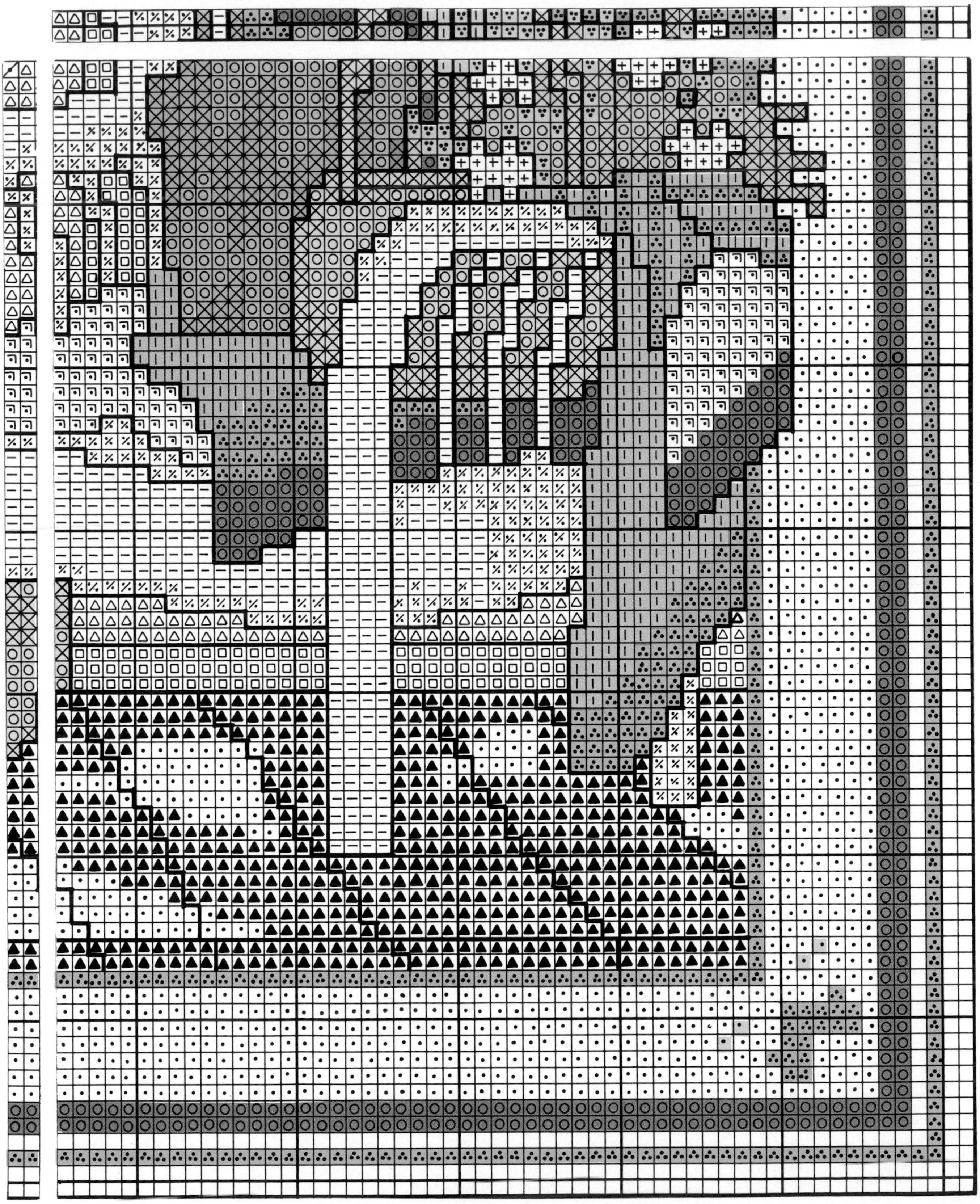

Country Bumpkins

Bear: Stitched on cream Belfast Linen 32 over 2 threads, the finished design size is 2⅜" x 2⅞". The fabric was cut 6" x 6".

FABRICS	DESIGN SIZES
Aida 11	3½" x 4⅛"
Aida 14	2¾" x 3¼"
Aida 18	2⅛" x 2½"
Hardanger 22	1¾" x 2⅛"

Rabbit: Stitched on cream Belfast Linen 32 over 2 threads, the finished design size is 1¾" x 2¾". The fabric was cut 6" x 6".

FABRICS	DESIGN SIZES
Aida 11	2⅝" x 4⅛"
Aida 14	2⅛" x 3¼"
Aida 18	1⅝" x 2½"
Hardanger 22	1⅜" x 2"

Anchor	DMC (used for sample)	
Step 1:	Cross-stitch (2 strands)	
292	3078	Golden Yellow-vy. lt.
886	677	Old Gold-vy. lt.
891	676	Old Gold-lt.
933	3774	Peach Pecan-med.
74	3354	Dusty Rose-vy. lt.
22	816	Garnet
168	807	Peacock Blue
921	931	Antique Blue-med.
882	407	Pecan
914	3772	Pecan-med.
936	632	Pecan-dk.
Step 2:	Backstitch (1 strand)	
936	632	Pecan-dk.
Step 3:	French knot (1 strand)	
936	632	Pecan-dk.

MATERIALS for one pillow

Completed cross-stitch design on cream Belfast Linen 32

⅛ yard of light lavender fabric; matching thread

½ yard of cream/lavender stripe fabric

Scraps of two coordinating lavender and cream check fabrics

Scrap each of dark lavender and light green fabric

1¼ yards of medium cording

One 14"-square pillow form

DIRECTIONS

1. Center and trim design piece to measure 4½" x 4½". From cream/lavender stripe fabric, cut one 12½" x 12½" piece for pillow back. From light lavender fabric, cut 1½"-wide bias strips, piecing as needed to equal 45". Make 45" inches of corded piping.

2. Choosing at random from remaining fabrics, cut the following pieces:

A:	4½" x 12½"
B:	4½" x 6½"
C & D:	8½" x 1½"
E & F:	2½" x 2½"
G:	4½" x 2½"
H:	4½" x 6½"

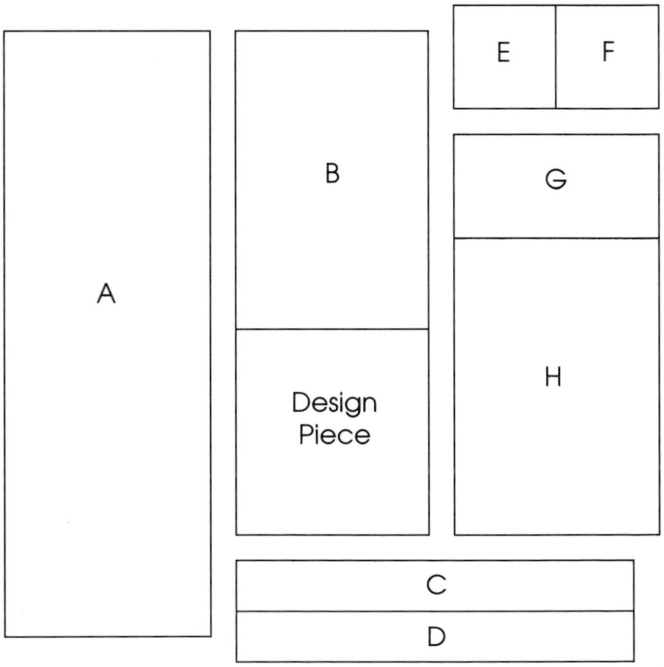

Diagram 1

3. With right sides facing, stitch pieces to form pillow front (Diagram 1).

4. With right sides facing and raw edges aligned, stitch corded piping to pillow front. Stitch pillow front to pillow back with right sides facing, leaving one edge open. Trim corners; turn. Insert pillow form; slipstitch opening closed.

Bear, Stitch Count: 38 x 46

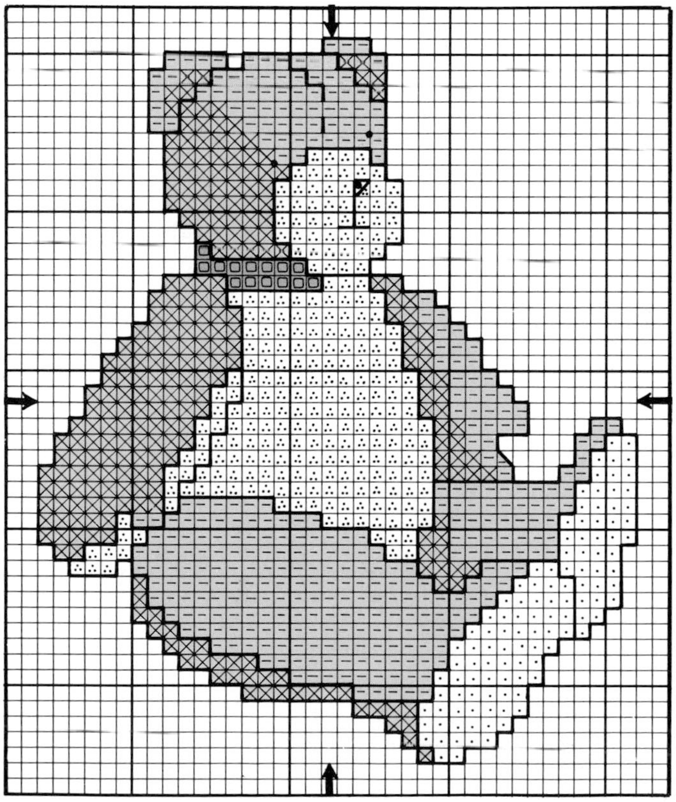

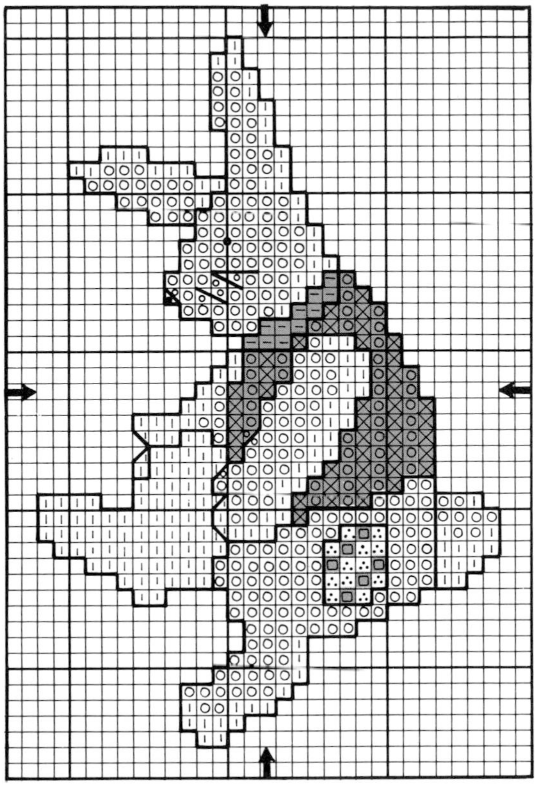

Bunny, Stitch Count: 29 x 45

Few sights stir the soul like one of Mother Nature's masterpieces—the magical rainbow. From out of the clouds, brilliant bands embrace the earth, renewing our belief in dreams just waiting to come true.

BUTTER
MY HEART LEAPS UP WHEN
I BEHOLD A RAINBOW IN THE SKY

Rainbow in the Sky

Stitched on cracked wheat Murano 30 over 2 threads, the finished design size is 13⅞" x 11¼". The fabric was cut 20" x 18".

FABRICS	DESIGN SIZES
Aida 11	18⅞" x 15⅜"
Aida 14	14⅞" x 12⅛"
Aida 18	11½" x 9⅜"
Hardanger 22	9½" x 7⅝"

Anchor	DMC (used for sample)	
Step 1: Cross-stitch (2 strands)		
1		White
386	746	Off White
886	677	Old Gold-vy. lt.
891	676	Old Gold-lt.
890	729	Old Gold-med.
933	3774	Peach Pecan-med.
881	945	Peach Beige
868	3779	Terra Cotta-vy. lt.
882	3773	Pecan-vy. lt.
10	3712	Salmon-med.
13	347	Salmon-vy. dk.
869	3743	Antique Violet-vy. lt.
158	3756	Baby Blue-ultra vy. lt.
160	3761	Sky Blue-lt.
167	3766	Peacock Blue-lt.
928	598	Turquoise-lt.
168	597	Turquoise
128	813	Blue-lt.
130	799	Delft-med.
920	932	Antique Blue-lt.
922	930	Antique Blue-dk.
900	928	Slate Green-lt.
779	926	Slate Green
213	369	Pistachio Green-vy. lt.
214	966	Baby Green-med.
210	562	Jade-med.
859	3052	Green Gray-med.
862	3362	Pine Green-dk.
363	436	Tan
370	434	Brown-lt.
900	648	Beaver Gray-lt.
401	844	Beaver Gray-ultra dk.
Step 2: Backstitch (1 strand)		
236	3799	Pewter Gray-vy. dk.
Step 3: French knot (1 strand)		
236	3799	Pewter Gray-vy. dk.

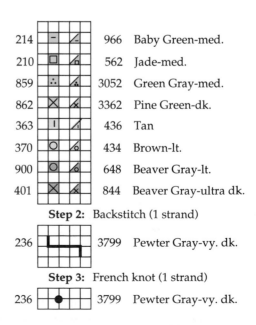

Stitch Count: 208 x 169

ART LEAPS UP

HEN

LD A RAINBOW IN THI

ESKY

Town and Country

Ark: The motif is from "Rainbow in the Sky." Stitched on white Jobelan 28 over 2 threads, the finished design size is 6⅜" x 2⅝". The stitch count is 89 x 36. The fabric was cut 12" x 20". Begin stitching in center of fabric.

Rainbow: The motif is from "Rainbow in the Sky." Stitched on white Jobelan 28 over 2 threads, the finished design size is 7⅛" x 3⅛". The stitch count is 99 x 43. The fabric was cut 18" x 19". Begin stitching in center of fabric.

Bunny: The motif is from "Rainbow in the Sky." Stitched on white Jobelan 28 over 2 threads, the finished design size is 2⅜" x 3⅝". Stitch five bunnies, ½" apart, with center bunny in center of fabric.

MATERIALS for ark pillow
Completed cross-stitch design on white Jobelan 28; matching thread
⅜ yard of unstitched white Jobelan 28
¼ yard of white satin
1¼ yards of ⅛"-wide cording
1¼ yards of 4½"-wide white flat eyelet
Two 1⅝"-wide covered button hardware sets
Stuffing

DIRECTIONS

1. Trim design piece to measure 9½" x 18½" with design centered. Cut two 6¼" x 18½" pieces for end bands from unstitched linen. From satin, cut 1¼"-wide bias strips, piecing as needed to equal 45". Make 45" of corded piping. Cut two 18½" lengths of eyelet.

2. Stitch corded piping to right side of design piece on long edges. Fold design piece with right sides facing and raw edges aligned; stitch 9½" edge. Turn. Fold band with right sides facing and short edges aligned; stitch short edge. Repeat.

3. Fold one eyelet piece with right sides facing and short edges aligned; stitch short edges. Turn. Slide eyelet over band, wrong side down, raw edges and seams aligned; baste. Repeat.

4. Stitch one band with eyelet to design piece, right sides facing. Repeat. Fold one raw edge of band ⅛" to wrong side; stitch gathering threads close to fold. Gather band; secure threads. Stuff firmly. Gather remaining band; secure threads. Cover buttons with satin following manufacturer's instructions. Sew buttons over the gathered bands.

MATERIALS for rainbow pillow
Completed cross-stitch design on white Jobelan 28; matching thread
⅛ yard of unstitched white Jobelan 28
¼ yard of white satin
1 yard of ⅛"-wide cording
2 yards of 4½"-wide white flat eyelet
Two 1⅝"-wide covered button hardware sets
Stuffing

DIRECTIONS

1. Trim design piece to measure 15½" x 17" with design centered. Cut two 3½" x 17" pieces from unstitched Jobelan for ends. From satin, cut 1¼"-wide bias strips, piecing as needed to equal 36". Make 36" of corded piping. Cut two 36" lengths from eyelet.

2. Stitch corded piping to right sides of design piece on long edges. Fold design piece to measure 7¾" x 17"; stitch the long edge. Turn.

3. Fold end with right sides facing and short edges aligned; stitch short edge. Repeat. Set aside.

4. Fold eyelet piece in half lengthwise, short edges aligned; stitch short edge. Turn. Then stitch gathering threads on raw edge. Gather to fit one long edge of end; baste with wrong side down. Repeat.

5. Stitch one end with eyelet to design piece, right sides facing, through all layers. Repeat. Fold one long edge ⅛" to wrong side of each end; stitch gathering threads close to fold. Repeat. Gather one end; secure threads. Stuff firmly. Gather remaining end; secure threads. Cover buttons with satin following manufacturer's instructions. Sew buttons over gathered ends.

MATERIALS for bunny pillow
Completed cross-stitch design on white Jobelan 28; matching thread
⅛ yard of unstitched white Jobelan 28
¼ yard of white satin
1 yard of ⅛"-wide cording
Two 1⅝"-wide covered button hardware set
Stuffing

DIRECTIONS
1. Trim design piece to measure 16" x 16" with design centered. Cut two 3" x 16" pieces from unstitched Jobelan for ends. From satin, cut 1¼"-wide bias strips, piecing as needed to equal 34". Make 34" of corded piping.

2. Stitch corded piping to right sides of design piece on side edges. Fold design piece with right sides facing and top and bottom edges aligned; stitch long edge. Turn.

3. Fold end with right sides facing and short edges aligned; stitch short edge. Stitch end to design piece with right sides facing. Fold ⅛" to wrong side on raw edge of end; stitch gathering threads close to fold. Repeat. Gather one end; secure threads. Stuff firmly. Gather remaining end; secure threads. Cover buttons with satin following manufacturer's instructions. Sew buttons over the gathered ends.

Time for a Catnap

The motif is from "Rainbow in the Sky." Stitched on Vanessa-Ann Afghan Weave 18 over two threads, the finished design size 3½" x 3½". The stitch count is 33 x 32. The fabric was cut 12½" x 12½". Stitch cat in center square, centered vertically with left edge 2¾" from decorative weave. Stitch two hearts ¼" apart with right edge of one heart ¾" from edge of decorative weave (see photo).

MATERIALS
Completed cross-stitch design on Vanessa-Ann Afghan Weave 18*
½ yard of dusty rose print fabric; matching thread
1½ yards of ¼"-wide cording
3½ yards of ⅛"-wide dusty rose silk ribbon*
Three ⅝"-wide cream ceramic heart buttons
Stuffing
*see Suppliers

DIRECTIONS
1. Cut one 12½" x 12½" piece from print fabric for back. Also cut 2"-wide bias strips, piecing as needed to equal 4 yards.

2. Fold bias strip lengthwise with wrong sides facing; stitch long edge. Thread cording through strip, gathering tightly as you go. Stitch cording to design piece, right sides facing and raw edges aligned.

3. Sew buttons centered in diamonds where weave intersects (see photo). Leaving 8" tails at beginning and end, weave ribbon through threads in pillow (see photo); tie tails in a bow.

4. Stitch design piece to back with right sides facing and raw edges aligned, sewing on stitching line of cording and leaving an opening. Trim corners. Turn. Stuff firmly. Slipstitch opening closed.

If you dare . . . spread a blanket in the shade of a tree, forget your cares and linger awhile. Sip on fresh-squeezed lemonade and waste the day, giving way to your daydreams. But don't forget . . . save a few for a rainy day.

Stitch Count: 144 x 118

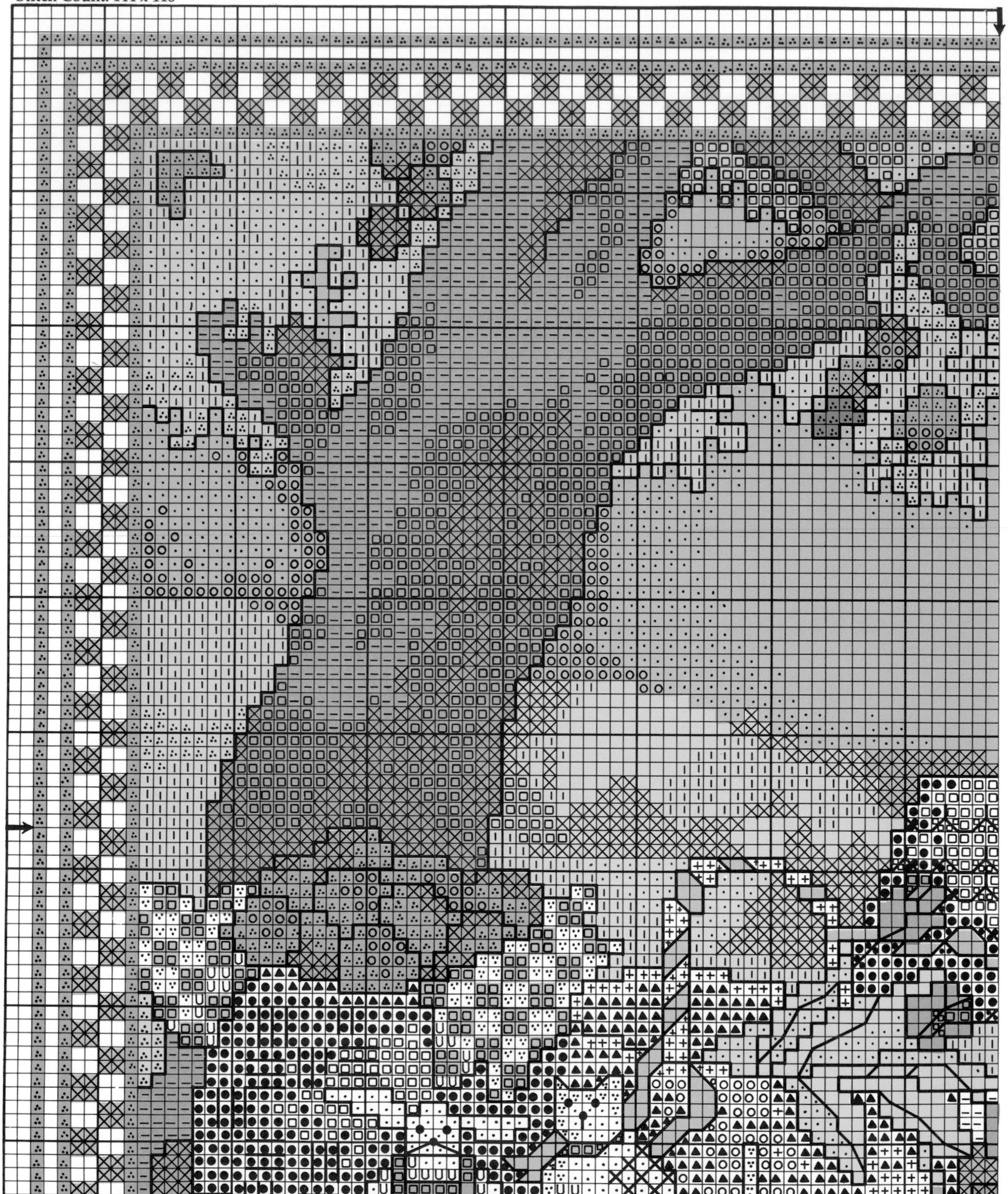

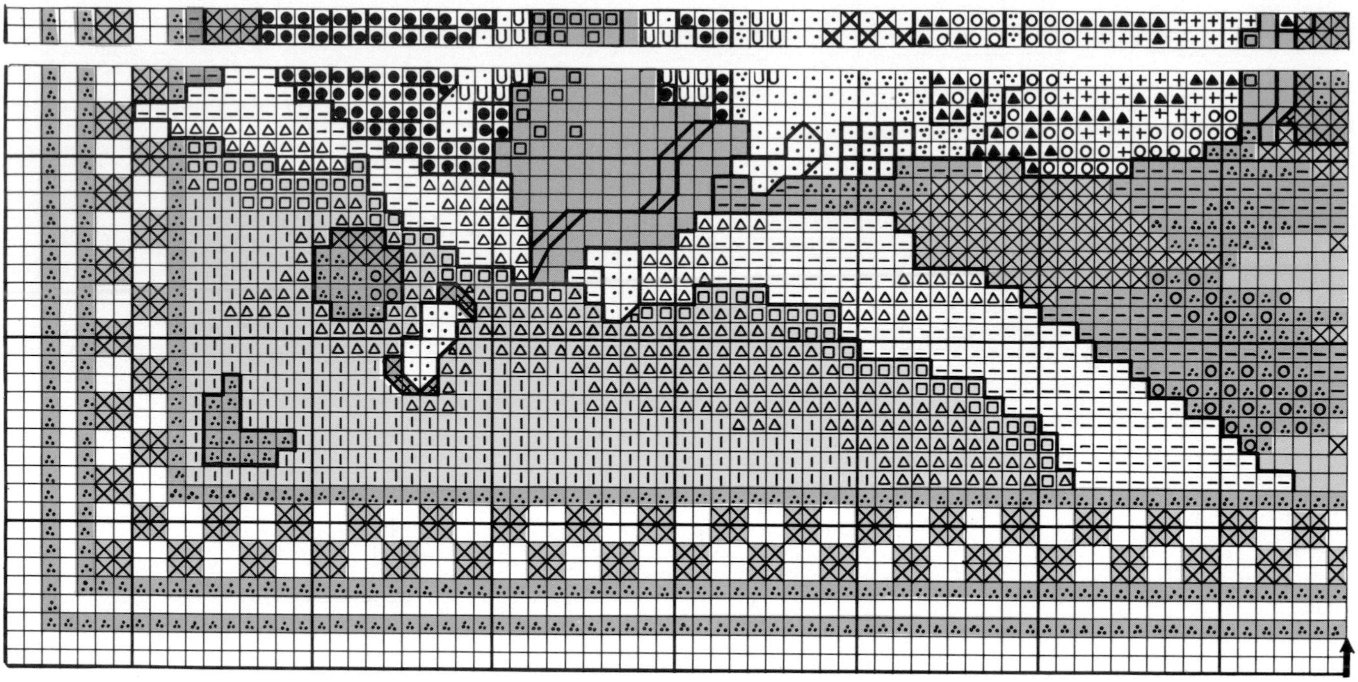

Summer Picnic

Stitched on cream Damask Aida 14 over 1 thread, the finished design size is 10¼" x 8⅜". The fabric was cut 17" x 15".

FABRICS	DESIGN SIZES
Aida 11	13⅛" x 10¾"
Aida 18	8" x 6½"
Hardanger 22	6½" x 5⅜"

Step 1: Cross-stitch (2 strands)

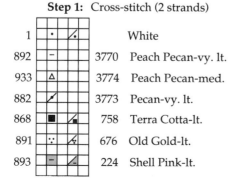

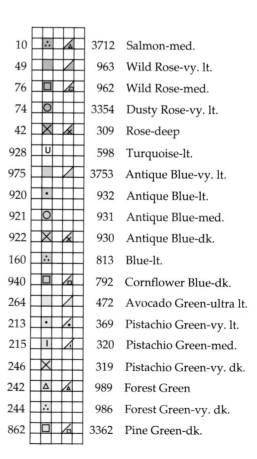

Anchor	Symbol	DMC (used for sample)	
1	•		White
892	–	3770	Peach Pecan-vy. lt.
933	△	3774	Peach Pecan-med.
882	/	3773	Pecan-vy. lt.
868	■	758	Terra Cotta-lt.
891	∵	676	Old Gold-lt.
893	–	224	Shell Pink-lt.
10	∴	3712	Salmon-med.
49		963	Wild Rose-vy. lt.
76	□	962	Wild Rose-med.
74	○	3354	Dusty Rose-vy. lt.
42	☒	309	Rose-deep
928	U	598	Turquoise-lt.
975		3753	Antique Blue-vy. lt.
920	•	932	Antique Blue-lt.
921	○	931	Antique Blue-med.
922	☒	930	Antique Blue-dk.
160	∴	813	Blue-lt.
940	□	792	Cornflower Blue-dk.
264		472	Avocado Green-ultra lt.
213	•	369	Pistachio Green-vy. lt.
215	ǀ	320	Pistachio Green-med.
246	☒	319	Pistachio Green-vy. dk.
242	△	989	Forest Green
244	∴	986	Forest Green-vy. dk.
862	□	3362	Pine Green-dk.

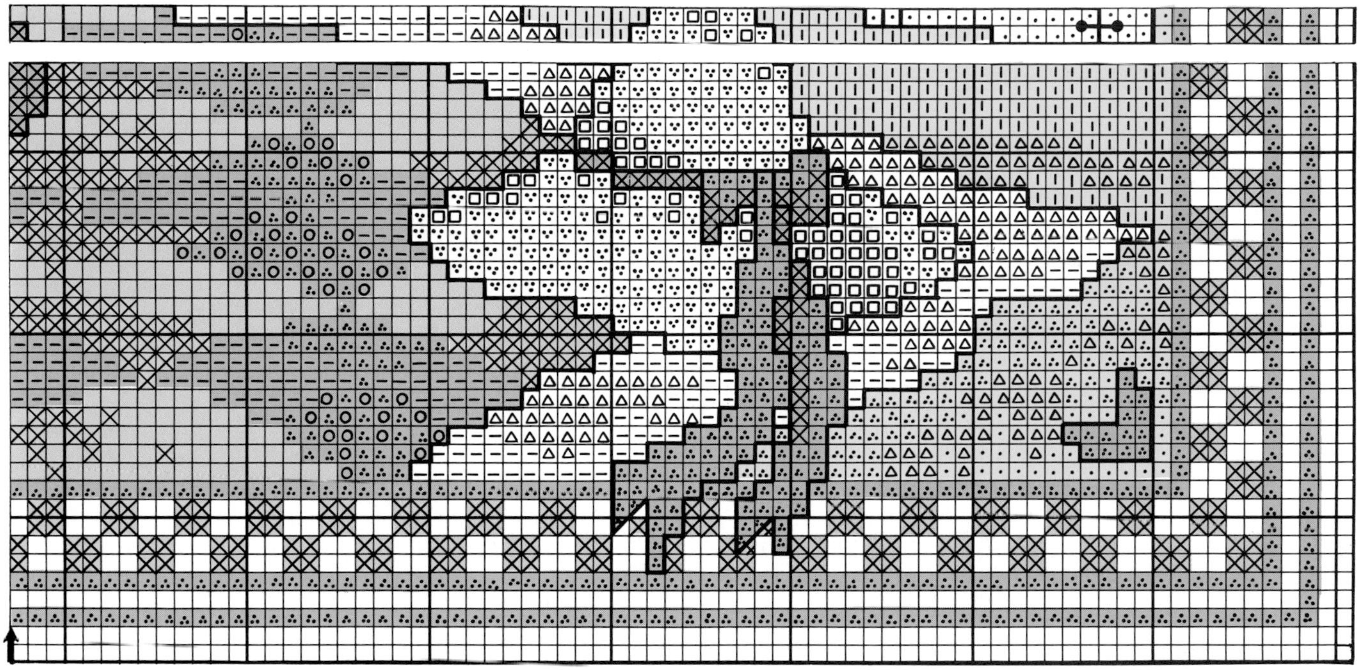

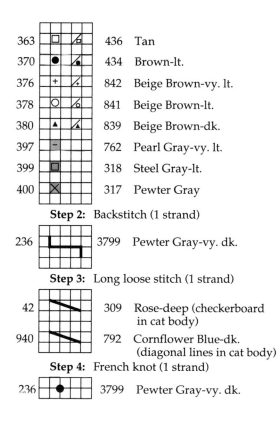

363	□	◿	436	Tan
370	●	◿	434	Brown-lt.
376	+	◿	842	Beige Brown-vy. lt.
378	○	◿	841	Beige Brown-lt.
380	▲	◿	839	Beige Brown-dk.
397	−		762	Pearl Gray-vy. lt.
399	▣		318	Steel Gray-lt.
400	✕		317	Pewter Gray

Step 2: Backstitch (1 strand)

236	⌐		3799	Pewter Gray-vy. dk.

Step 3: Long loose stitch (1 strand)

42	╱		309	Rose-deep (checkerboard in cat body)
940	╱		792	Cornflower Blue-dk. (diagonal lines in cat body)

Step 4: French knot (1 strand)

236	●		3799	Pewter Gray-vy. dk.

Swingin' in Summertime

Doll dress: Stitched on amaretto Murano 30 over 2 threads, the finished design size is 2¾" x 2¼". The fabric was cut 10" x 7".

Heart strip: Stitched on amaretto Murano 30 over 2 threads, the finished design size for each heart is ⅝" x ⅝". Stitch seven hearts, ¼" apart. The fabric was cut 8" x 3" .

FABRICS	**DESIGN SIZES** Doll dress	**DESIGN SIZES** Heart strip
Aida 11	3⅞" x 3"	⅞" x ⅞"
Aida 14	3" x 2⅜"	¾" x ¾"
Aida 18	2⅜" x 1⅞"	½" x ½"
Hardanger 22	1⅞" x 1½"	½" x ½"

Step 1: Cross-stitch (2 strands)

Anchor	Symbol	**DMC (used for sample)**	
886	□	677	Old Gold-vy. lt.
893	I	224	Shell Pink-lt.
10	O	3712	Salmon-med.
42	X	335	Rose
920	■	932	Antique Blue-lt.
264	–	772	Pine Green-lt.

Step 2: Backstitch (1 strand)

Anchor	Symbol	**DMC (used for sample)**	
920	backstitch line	932	Antique Blue-lt.

Stitch Count: 9 x 9

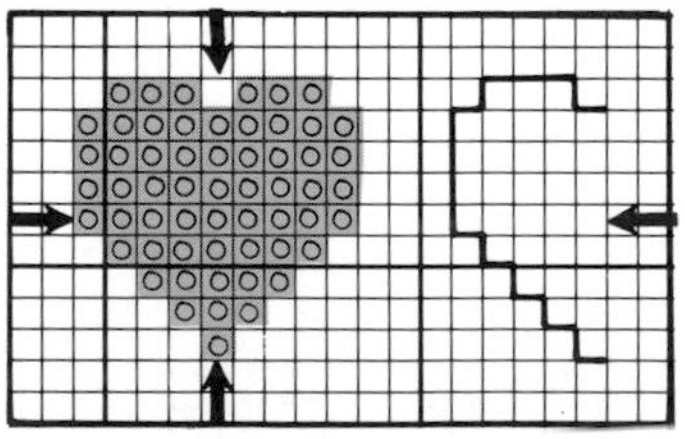

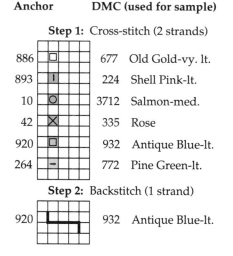

MATERIALS for doll

Completed cross-stitch design on amaretto Murano 30; matching thread
Scrap of unstitched amaretto Murano 30
One scrap each of peach and white fabrics; matching threads
¾ yard of 1⅛"-wide blue satin ribbon
¼ yard of 1"-wide white eyelet lace
4 yards of pale yellow acrylic yarn
Stuffing
Masking tape
One cup of birdseed
10" of 16-gauge wire

DIRECTIONS

1. Place dress pattern over design piece, centering design vertically; cut.

2. From unstitched Murano, cut one dress and two hats. Cut two bodies and four legs from peach fabric. Cut two slips from white fabric. Cut one 8¾", one 14", and two 3¼" lengths from ribbon. Cut one 8" length from eyelet.

3. To make body, stitch bodies with right sides facing, leaving an opening (see pattern). Clip curves and corners; turn. Stuff head and arms firmly with stuffing. Bend wire in hairpin shape, taping ends; insert in body

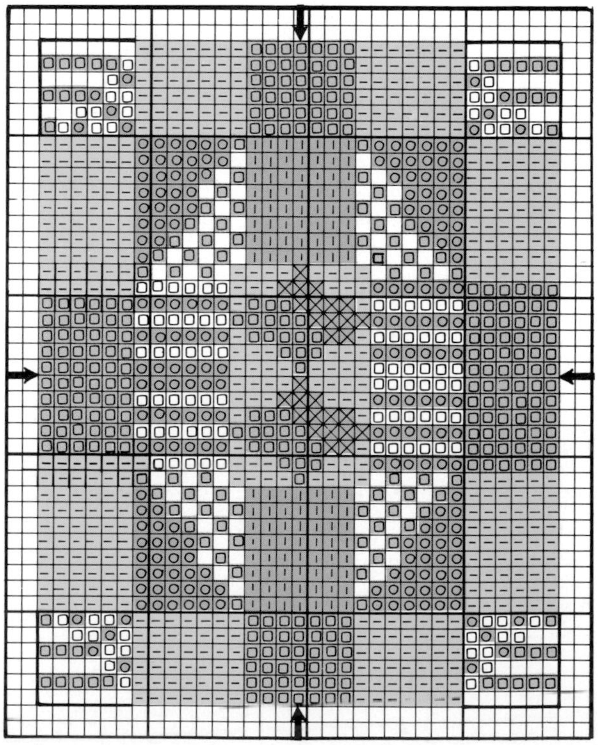

Stitch Count: 33 x 42

across shoulders. To form hands, wrap thread tightly ½" from end of each arm; secure. Fill body with birdseed; baste opening. To make leg, stitch two legs with right sides facing, leaving top edge open. Clip curves; turn. Fill with birdseed; baste opening. Repeat. Carefully remove basting threads in opening of body. Place legs in opening with seams centered in front and back; stitch opening closed.

4. To make slip, stitch slips at shoulder and side seams, right sides facing. Zigzag neck and arm holes. Turn. Stitch ends of 8" length of eyelet together, right sides facing. Sew to bottom of slip with right sides facing and raw edges aligned.

5. To make dress, stitch design piece to unstitched Murano dress at shoulder and side seams, right sides facing. Zigzag neck and bottom edges of sleeves; then fold ¼" to wrong side. Sew gathering threads close to folds. Sew ¼" hem on bottom edge of dress. Slipstitch 8¾" length of ribbon ¼" above bottom edge of dress and one 3¼" length ⅜" from bottom edge of each sleeve.

6. Place slip and dress on doll. Gather neck and sleeves tightly; secure.

7. Make ringlets using yarn (see General Instructions). Fold and tack along seam of head, clipping as desired (see photo).

8. To make hat, stitch hats with right sides facing, leaving an opening. Clip corners; turn. Slipstitch opening closed. Sew gathering threads from inner point to inner point (see pattern). Place hat on doll. Gather to fit head; secure threads. Tack hat to neck seams and center back of head. Tie ribbon in a bow around neck over gathering threads.

MATERIALS for hearts
Completed cross-stitch design on Murano 30
Scrap of unstitched Murano 30
Scrap each of the following fabrics: blue, rust, blue print, mauve print, rust print
¾ yard of ⅛"-wide blue satin ribbon
¾ yard of ⅛"-wide cording
Cream thread
Stuffing

DIRECTIONS

1. Trim design piece to measure 1¼" x 8½".

2. From unstitched Murano, cut one each of hearts B, C and D. Also from Murano cut three 8½"-long strips, varying in width from 1" to 1¼". Repeat with each scrap except blue. From blue fabric, cut 1½"-wide bias strips, piecing as needed to equal 27". Make 27" of corded tubing (see General instructions). Cut one 2½", one 3½" and one 4½" length from ribbon.

3. Join four different strips and design piece with right sides facing on long edges, placing design piece near center (see photo). Cut one right side of heart A, adding ¼" to straight edge (see pattern).

4. Join remaining strips with right sides facing on long edges. Cut one heart A and one heart B vertically. Cut one left side of heart A, adding ¼" on straight edge, one heart C and one heart D horizontally.

5. To make large heart, with right sides facing, stitch left and right sides of heart A. Stitch the two heart As together, leaving an opening. Turn. Stuff firmly. Slipstitch opening closed.

6. To make small hearts, stitch Murano heart B to pieced heart with right sides facing, leaving an opening. Turn. Stuff firmly. Slipstitch opening closed. Repeat for hearts C and D. Make a 1¼" loop at end of each ribbon. Tack one ribbon loop to cleavage of each small heart. Treating all ribbons as one unit, tie in a bow. Set aside.

7. Knot ends of corded tubing. Tack knots 1" from top and sides on back of large heart.

8. Place doll on cleavage of large heart. Tack hands to tubing and dress hem to back of heart. Tack bow/hearts to doll hand (see photo).

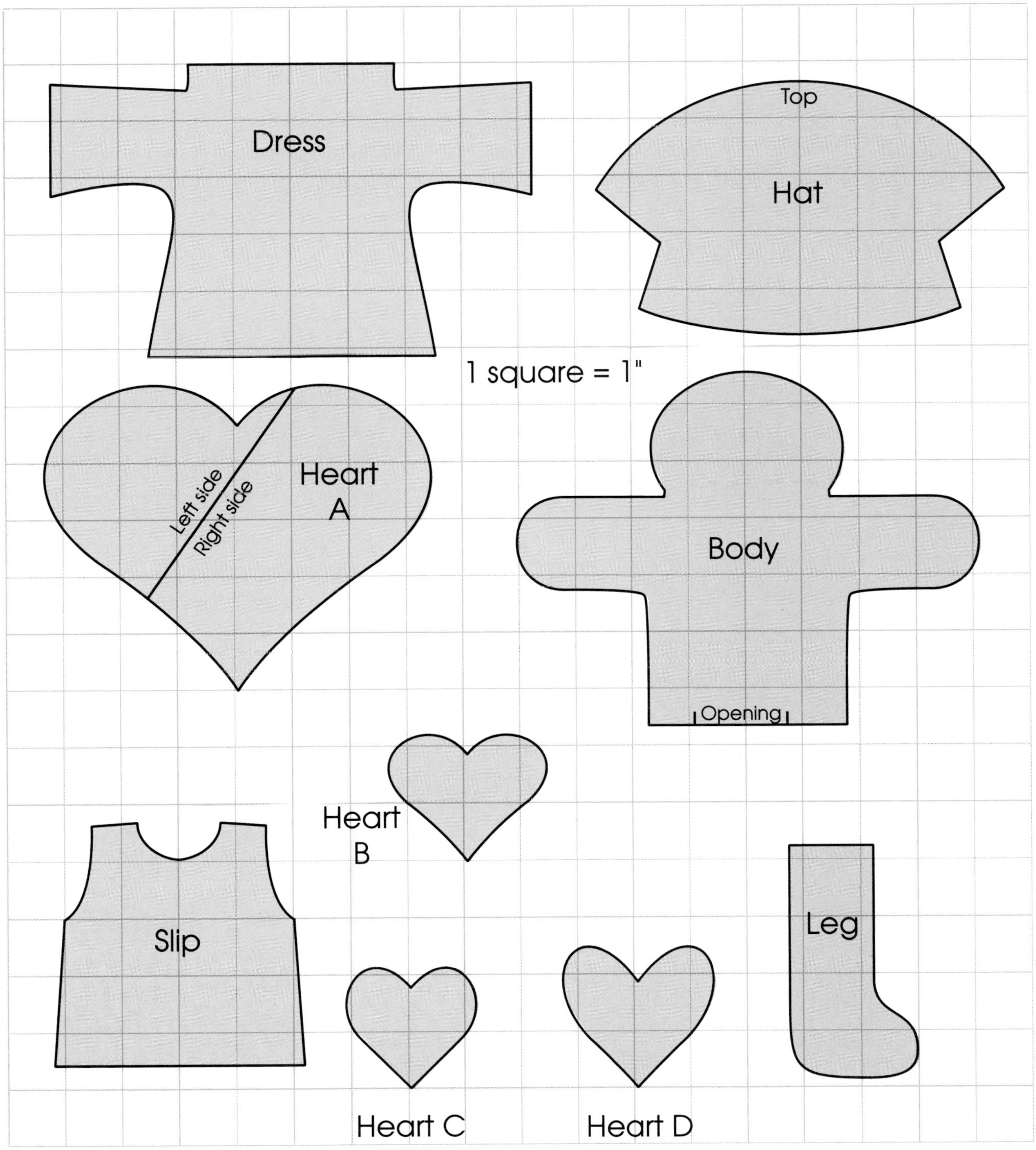
Dress
Top
Hat
1 square = 1"
Left side
Right side
Heart
A
Body
Opening
Heart
B
Slip
Leg
Heart C
Heart D

It is only with the heart
that one can see rightly

From our hearts come life's finest memories. They're old-fashioned, yes, but timeless. Rediscover cherished memories as you stitch these visions of the heart.

Only with the Heart

Stitched on cream Pastel Linen 28 over 2 threads, the finished design size is 14⅝" x 11¾". The fabric was cut 21" x 18".

FABRICS	DESIGN SIZES
Aida 11	18½" x 15"
Aida 14	14⅝" x 11¾"
Aida 18	11⅜" x 9⅛"
Hardanger 22	9¼" x 7½"

Anchor **DMC (used for sample)**

Step 1: Cross-stitch (2 strands)

Anchor	Symbol	DMC	Color
1	△		White
386	−	746	Off White
292	✕	3078	Golden Yellow-vy. lt.
886	U	677	Old Gold-vy. lt.
891	•	676	Old Gold-lt.
890	●	729	Old Gold-med.
881	□	945	Peach Beige
347	∴	402	Mahogany-vy. lt.
881	/	3779	Terra Cotta-vy. lt.
868	○	758	Terra Cotta-lt.
337	▲	3778	Terra Cotta
914	■	3772	Pecan-med.
8	•	761	Salmon-lt.
9	□	760	Salmon
10	○	3712	Salmon-med.
49	|	963	Wild Rose-vy. lt.
74	△	3354	Dusty Rose-vy. lt.
59	✕	326	Rose-vy. dk.
870	○	3042	Antique Violet-lt.
871	✕	3041	Antique Violet-med.
160	□	813	Blue-lt.
975	•	3753	Antique Blue-vy. lt.
921	△	931	Antique Blue-med.
922	✕	930	Antique Blue-dk.
779	○	926	Slate Green
214	−	966	Baby Green-med.
875	•	503	Blue Green-med.
210	▽	562	Jade-med.
212	✕	561	Jade-vy. dk.
862	□	3362	Pine Green-dk.
887	U	372	Mustard-lt.
309	+	435	Brown-vy. lt.
379	+	840	Beige Brown-med.
900	∴	648	Beaver Gray-lt.
397	|	762	Pearl Gray-vy. lt.

Step 2: Backstitch (1 strand)

Anchor	DMC	Color
236	3799	Pewter Gray-vy. dk.

Step 3: French knot (1 strand)

Anchor	DMC	Color
236	3799	Pewter Gray-vy. dk.

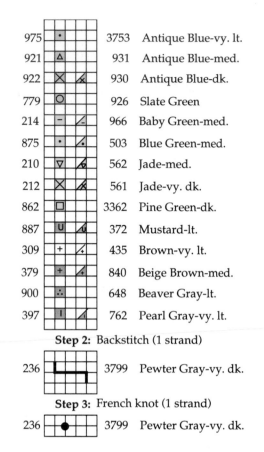

Stitch Count: 204 x 165

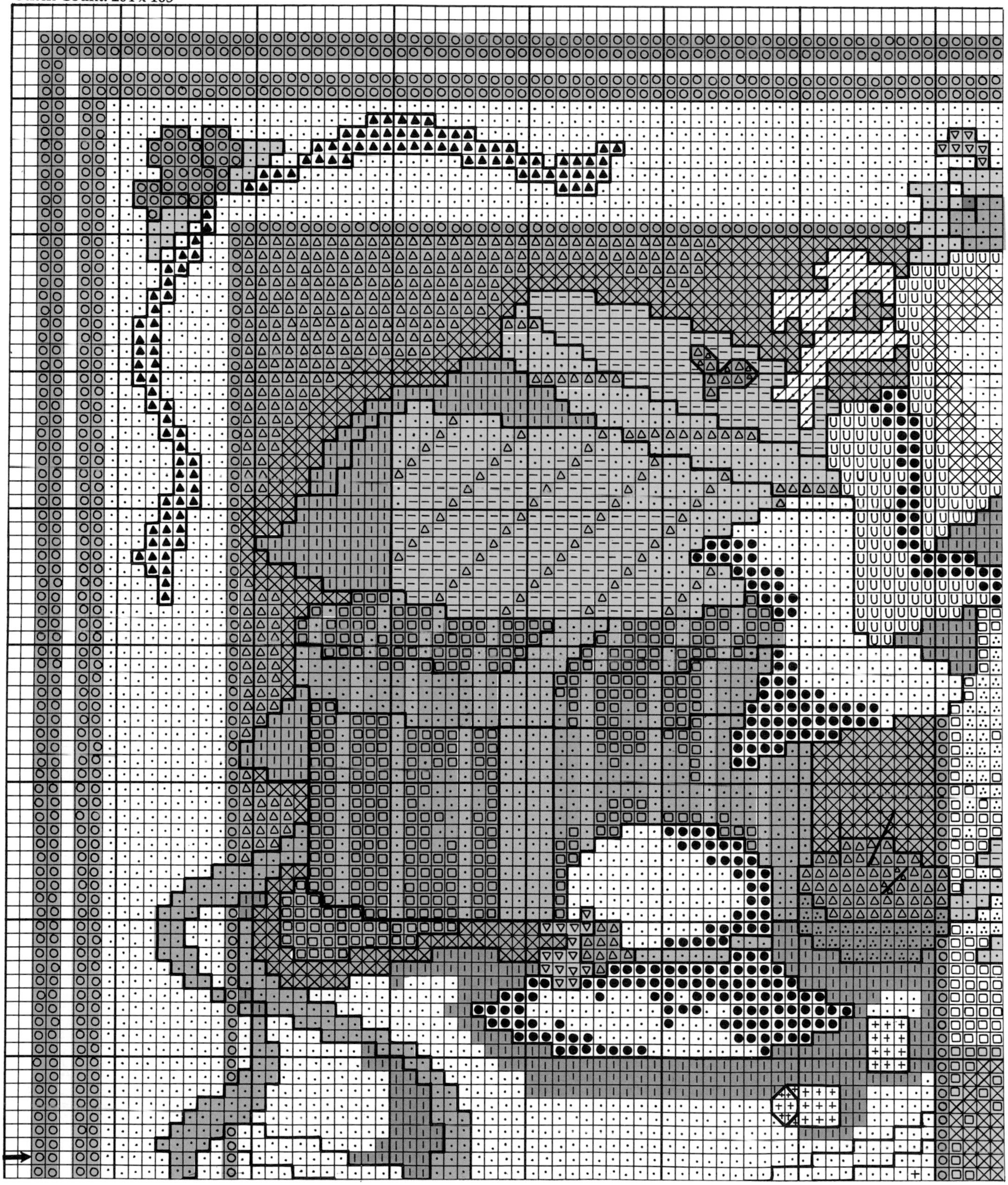

It is only with the heart
that one can see rightly

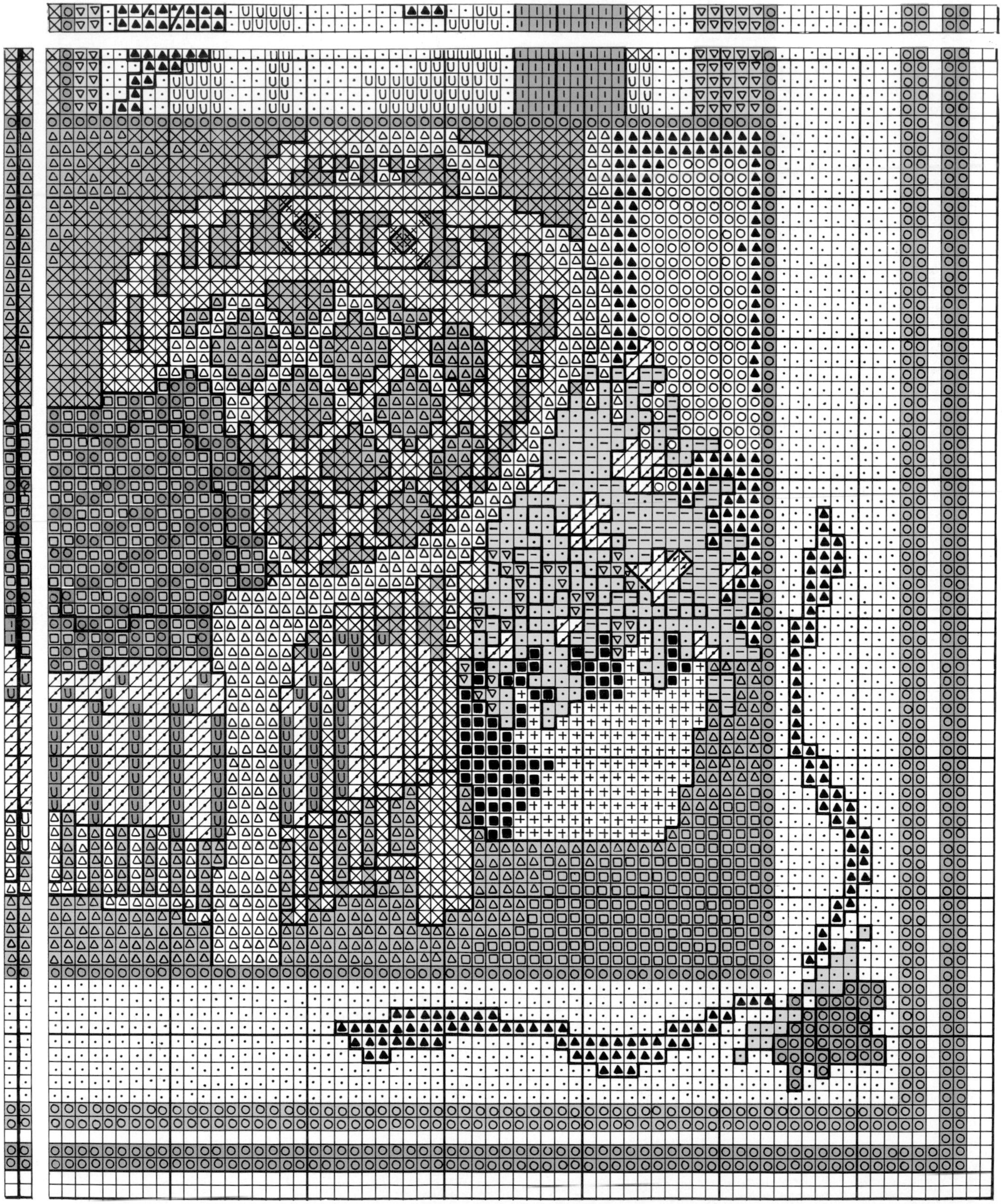

Gloriously Scented Goose

The motif is from "Only with the Heart." Stitched on cream Belfast Linen 32 over 2 threads, the finished design size is 2½" x 2". The stitch count is 40 x 30. The fabric was cut 8" x 6" for one. Cut and stitch two design pieces.

MATERIALS

Completed cross-stitch designs on cream Belfast Linen 32; matching thread
¼ yard of unstitched cream Belfast Linen 32
¼ yard of lightweight fusible interfacing
⅛ yard of cream satin
Two 2"-wide circles of muslin
20" of each of the following ribbons: light green satin, pink satin, rose picot
1 yard of ⅛" cording
¼ cup of potpourri (see General Instructions)
Stuffing
Fleece

DIRECTIONS

1. Place wing pattern over one design piece with four flowers centered in widest end (see photo); cut. Repeat for second wing.

2. From unstitched linen, cut two bodies, two wings and one gusset. From interfacing, cut two bodies, four wings and one gusset. From fleece, cut two wings. Cut 1¼"-wide bias strips from satin, piecing as needed to equal 36". Make 36" of corded piping.

3. Fuse interfacing to wrong side of one design piece and one unstitched wing following manufacturer's directions. Stitch piping to right side of design piece. Pin fleece wing to wrong side of unstitched wing. With right sides facing, stitch design piece and unstitched wing together, leaving a small opening. Turn. Slipstitch opening closed. Repeat for second wing.

4. Stitch darts in body pieces (see pattern). With right sides facing, stitch body pieces together from neck (A), then around head to tail (B), backstitching at marks (see pattern). Stitch body and gusset together with right sides facing, leaving an opening; backstitch. Turn.

5. To make potpourri pouch, stitch muslin circles together, leaving an opening. Fill with potpourri. Slipstitch opening closed. Stuff tail with potpourri pouch. Stuff rest of goose firmly with stuffing. Slipstitch opening closed. Slipstitch wings to body (see photo). Handling ribbons as one, tie a bow around goose neck.

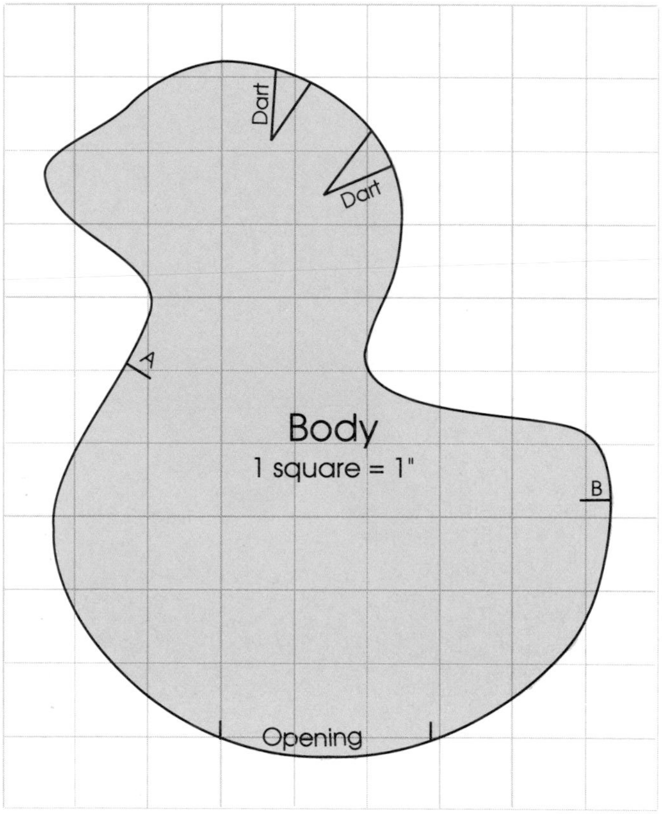

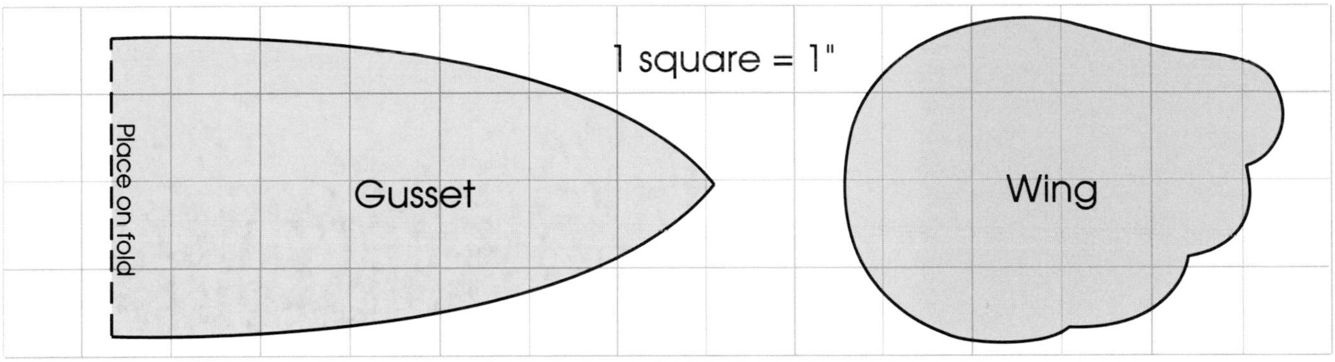

Served in Style

The motif is from "Only with the Heart." Stitched on mocha Dublin Linen 25 over 2 threads, the finished design size is 5⅞" x 5⅜". The stitch count is 73 x 67. The fabric was cut 20" x 14".

MATERIALS

Completed cross-stitch design on mocha Dublin Linen 25
½ yard of 3⁄16"-wide lavender silk ribbon;* matching thread
½ yard of 1"-wide light green satin ribbon; matching thread
1½ yards each of ⅛"-wide burgundy and pink silk ribbons*
Two handles (available at home improvement stores)
One 18" x 12" piece of black felt
Glue gun and glue
One 17⅜" x 11⅜" frame; see Step 2
*see Suppliers

DIRECTIONS

1. Beginning at one short edge, slipstitch lavender ribbon horizontally to right side of design piece, aligned with red stitching on bottom of basket so that basket appears to sit on ribbon. Weave ribbon under red stitching. Slipstitch light green ribbon parallel to and 1" from lavender ribbon.

2. Cut the burgundy and pink ribbons into 18" lengths. Treating the lengths as one, tie in a bow. Glue bow to base of basket handle, shaping tails as desired (see photo). Have design piece professionally framed, centering design horizontally just below center of frame. Glue felt on back of frame; trim excess. Center and attach handles to each side (see photo).

The coming of dawn promises a fresh beginning, a new day to work and dream, to love and laugh. Welcome each new day with images from the "good life"—yours.

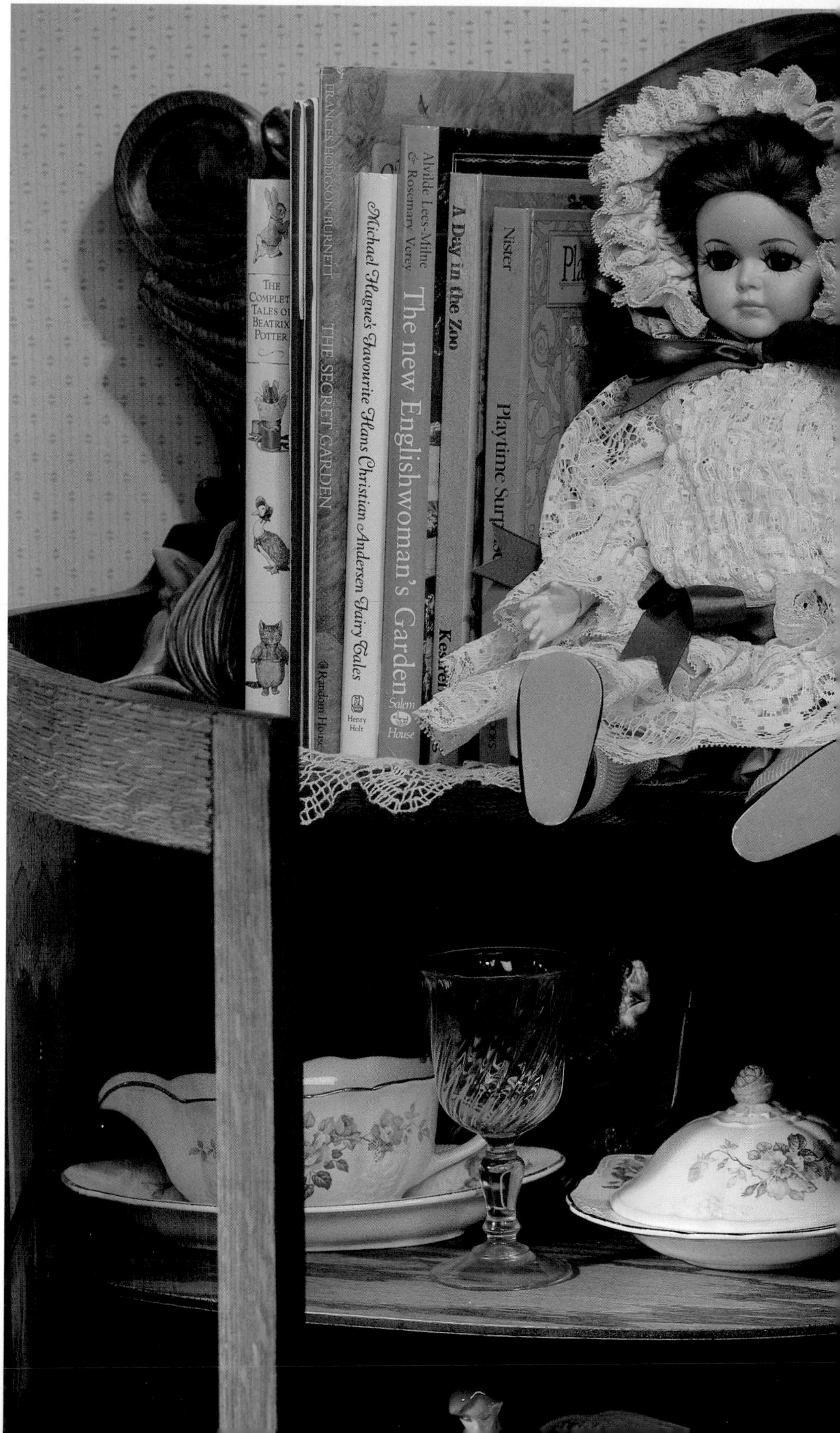

WELCOME EACH NEW DAY

Welcome Each New Day

Stitched on cream Aida 14 over 1 thread, the finished design size is 12½" x 10¼". The fabric was cut 19" x 17".

FABRICS	DESIGN SIZES
Aida 11	15⅞" x 13⅛"
Aida 18	9¾" x 8"
Hardanger 22	8" x 6½"

Step 1: Cross-stitch (2 strands)

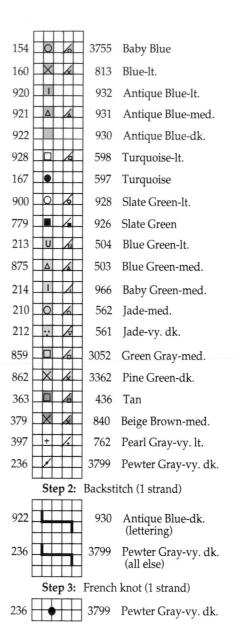

Anchor	Symbol	DMC (used for sample)	Color
1	•		White
386	Δ	746	Off White
292	U	3078	Golden Yellow-vy. lt.
886	∴	677	Old Gold-vy. lt.
891	X	676	Old Gold-lt.
890	▲	729	Old Gold-med.
933	–	3774	Peach Pecan-med.
882	I	407	Pecan
914	Δ	3772	Pecan-med.
893	–	224	Shell Pink-lt.
10	X	3712	Salmon-med.
13	∴	347	Salmon-vy. dk.
343	•	3752	Antique Blue-ultra vy. lt.
154	O	3755	Baby Blue
160	X	813	Blue-lt.
920	I	932	Antique Blue-lt.
921	Δ	931	Antique Blue-med.
922		930	Antique Blue-dk.
928	□	598	Turquoise-lt.
167	●	597	Turquoise
900	O	928	Slate Green-lt.
779	■	926	Slate Green
213	U	504	Blue Green-lt.
875	Δ	503	Blue Green-med.
214	I	966	Baby Green-med.
210	O	562	Jade-med.
212	∵	561	Jade-vy. dk.
859	□	3052	Green Gray-med.
862	X	3362	Pine Green-dk.
363	□	436	Tan
379	X	840	Beige Brown-med.
397	+	762	Pearl Gray-vy. lt.
236	/	3799	Pewter Gray-vy. dk.

Step 2: Backstitch (1 strand)

Anchor	DMC	Color
922	930	Antique Blue-dk. (lettering)
236	3799	Pewter Gray-vy. dk. (all else)

Step 3: French knot (1 strand)

Anchor	DMC	Color
236	3799	Pewter Gray-vy. dk.

Stitch Count: 175 x 144

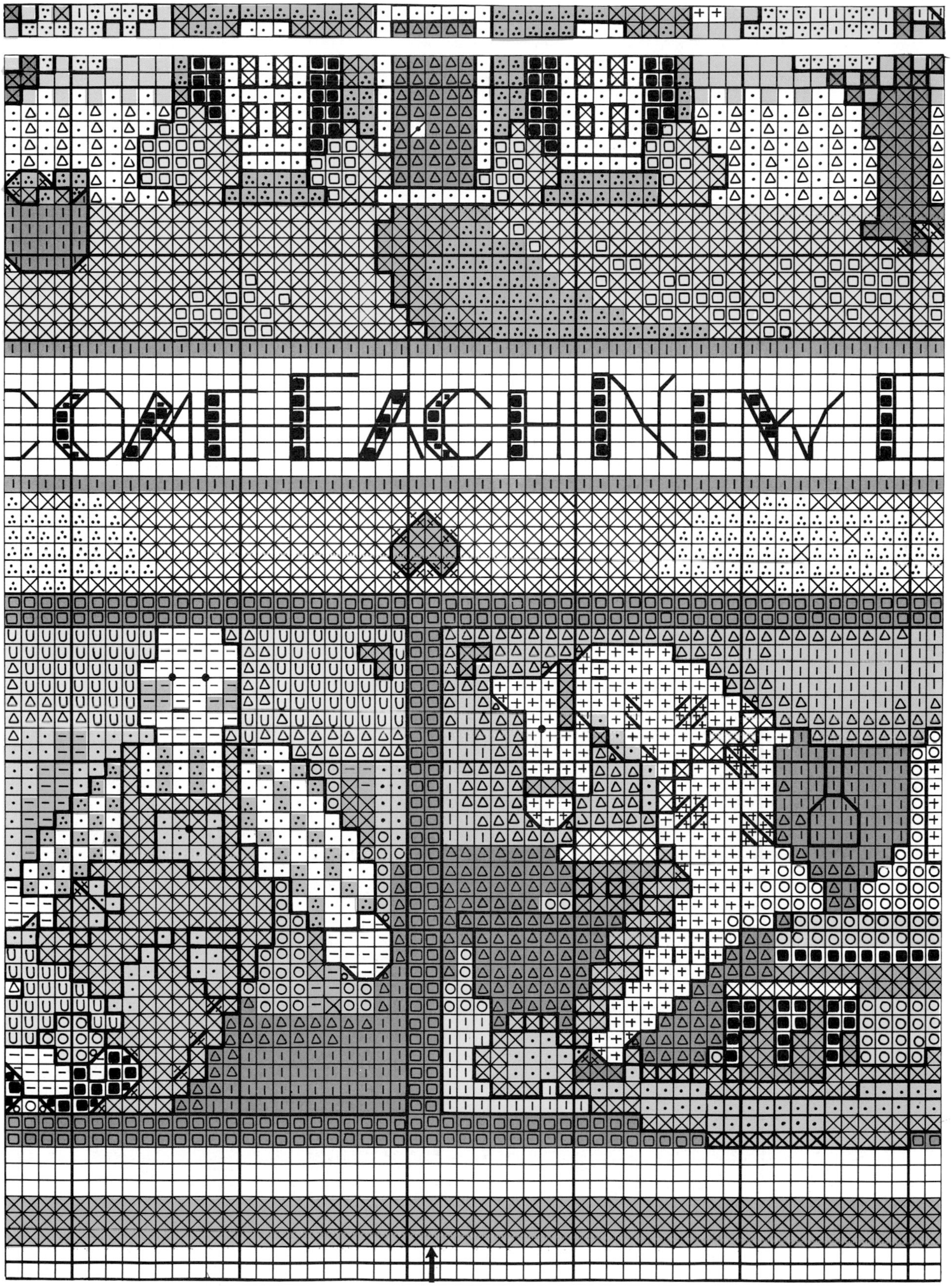

Apple Sense

Stitched on khaki Linda 27 over 2 threads, the finished design size is 2⅛" x 2⅛". The fabric was cut 6" x 6".

FABRICS	DESIGN SIZES
Aida 11	2¾" x 2⅝"
Aida 14	2⅛" x 2⅛"
Aida 18	1⅝" x 1⅝"
Hardanger 22	1⅜" x 1⅜"

Anchor **DMC (used for sample)**

Step 1: Cross-stitch (2 strands)

Anchor	Symbol	DMC	Color
292	X	3078	Golden Yellow-vy. lt.
22	O	816	Garnet
161	∴	826	Blue-med.
849	□	927	Slate Green
779	●	926	Slate Green-med.
862	X	3362	Pine Green-dk.
914	O	3772	Pecan-med.

MATERIALS for wreath
Juice from 15 lemons
5 teaspoons salt
24 large firm apples (Rome Reds or Ida Reds preferred)
8 ounces of ground cinnamon
4 ounces of ground allspice
4 ounces of ground cloves
One 10"-diameter round wire frame or 33" of heavy-gauge wire
Floral tape
Floral wire
Sharp knife
Paper towels
Two bowls
Small sieve, tea strainer or sifter
Pastry brush
Broiler pan or wire screen
Pliers
Scissors
Spray bottle (optional)

DIRECTIONS
1. To make wreath, blend lemon juice and salt in bowl. Slice apples horizontally into ⅛"-thick round slices. Remove seeds. Steep slices in lemon juice for 6 minutes, turning once. Place slices on paper towels; pat dry.

2. Blend spices in bowl. Dust apple slices well with spices, using sieve. Gently remove excess spice with pastry brush. Turn slices and dust again.

3. Place apple slices in a single layer on broiler pan or wire screen. Dry in conventional oven at 150°-200° for three hours or until slightly pliable. For microwave, dry slices 4-6 minutes at low to medium power.

4. To make one apple rose, roll one slice to form center by overlapping ends ⅛". Stagger 11-12 slices around center at overlapping intervals. Wrap floral tape carefully around bottom of rose. Then carefully wrap floral wire around tape to secure, leaving long ends for attaching. (Wrapping too tightly will cut the rose.) Repeat to make five roses. Make two buds, following procedure above and using seven slices per bud. Return roses to oven on warm setting until practically dry. (If slices get too dry, spray with fine mist.) Set aside roses and buds.

5. Straighten hooked ends of the round frame with pliers. Or, using 33" of wire, make a 10"-diameter circle. Thread remaining apple slices on frame until completely covered. Using pliers, bend ends of wire back to make hooks; re-connect to close wreath. Attach roses and buds to wreath (see photo).

MATERIALS for ornament
Completed cross-stitch design on khaki Linda 27; matching thread
One 4" x 4" piece of unstitched khaki Linda 27
3½ yards of each color of floss (see code)
Stuffing

DIRECTIONS
1. Trim design piece to 4" x 4" with design centered.

2. To make ornament, stitch design piece to unstitched Linda with right sides facing, leaving an opening. Clip the corners. Turn. Stuff firmly. Slipstitch opening closed.

3. Using 3½ yard strands of each color of floss, tie a knot 1" from end; braid. Leaving 7" tails at beginning and end, slipstitch braid to ornament seam. Knot and fray ends of each tail, then tie tails in a bow on one side (see photo). Cut one 44" and two 24" pieces from remaining braid. Knot and fray all ends. Thread 44" piece through center top of braid on ornament for hanger. Tie ornament to wreath (see photo).

Stitch Count: 30 x 28

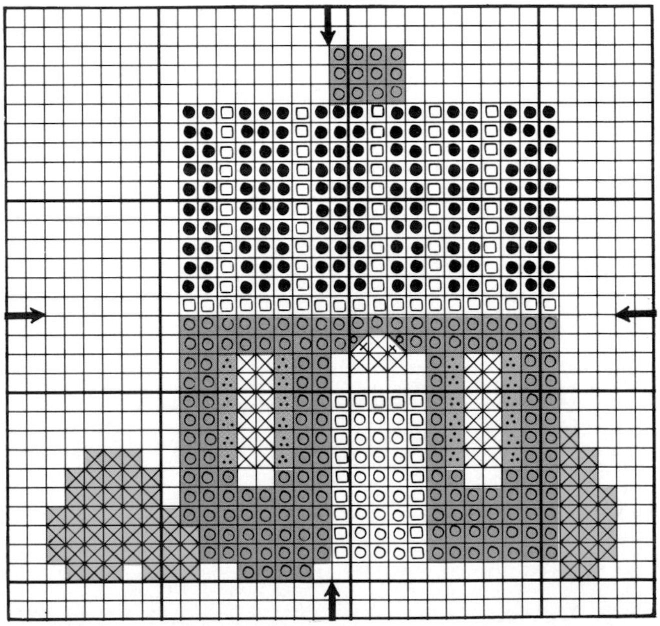

Comforts of Home

MATERIALS

Yarn description: Sportweight wool silk blend, Natural; Persian yarns (see code for colors)

Yarn pictured: Classic Elite Acadia, 50-gr., 115-yard skeins, 15 skeins Natural #2116; Paternayan Persian Yarns* (see code for colors)

Tools: Afghan crochet hook size F, approximate length 14"; crochet hook size F; one large-eyed needle

*see Suppliers

GAUGE

Afghan st:
19 sts = 4"
13 rows = 3"

DIRECTIONS

Center panel (make 1): With size F afghan hook, ch 62. Work afghan st for 144 rows. When piece totals 62 x 144 blocks, bind off.

Side panel (make 2): With size F afghan hook, ch 20. Work afghan st for 144 rows. When piece totals 20 x 144 blocks, bind off.

Single crochet: Work one row of sc around ea panel, work one sc in ea block and 3 sc in ea corner, end with sl st in first sc worked.

Lace panel (make 2): Ch 25, loosely.

Row 1: Ch 3 for beg dc, [2 dc, ch 2, 2 dc (shell)] in 4th ch from hook, sk next 2 sts, * [dc, ch 2, dc (v-st)] in next st, sk next 2 sts, shell in next st, sk next 2 sts, rep from * across, end with dc in last st, turn.

Row 2: Ch 3 for beg dc, shell in next ch-2 sp, * v-st in next ch 2 sp, shell in next ch-2 sp, rep from * across, end with dc in top ch of ch, turn.

Cont to rep row 2 until piece measures same length as afghan stitch panel (approximately 54 rows).

Assembly of panels: With matching yarn threaded in a large-eyed needle, slipstitch the lace panels between the afghan-stitch panels.

Ruffle border: Rnd 1: Join yarn in any corner sc, ch 3 for first dc, (dc, ch 2, 2 dc) in same st, (sk next 2 sc, shell in next sc) around, sl st to top of beg ch-3.

Rnd 2: Sl st in next dc and into center ch-2 sp of same shell, ch 3 for first dc, (dc, ch 2, 2 dc) in same sp, * shell bet shells, * * shell in ch-2 sp in center of next shell, rep from * around, end last rep at * *, sl st to top of beg ch-3. Fasten off.

Cross-stitch: Stitch on crocheted afghan. The finished design sizes are: side panel, 3¼" x 32½"; center panel, 14" x 32½". Begin stitching at center of each panel. Repeat side panel graph on both side panels of afghan.

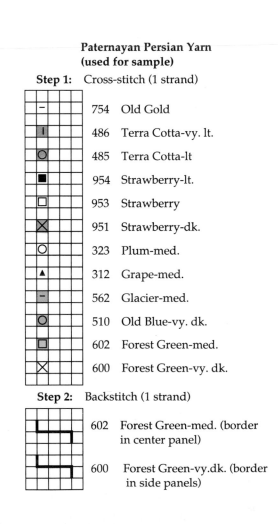

Paternayan Persian Yarn (used for sample)

Step 1: Cross-stitch (1 strand)

Symbol	No.	Color
–	754	Old Gold
| (shaded)	486	Terra Cotta-vy. lt.
○ (shaded)	485	Terra Cotta-lt
■	954	Strawberry-lt.
□	953	Strawberry
☒ (shaded)	951	Strawberry-dk.
○	323	Plum-med.
▲	312	Grape-med.
– (shaded)	562	Glacier-med.
○ (shaded)	510	Old Blue-vy. dk.
□ (shaded)	602	Forest Green-med.
☒	600	Forest Green-vy. dk.

Step 2: Backstitch (1 strand)

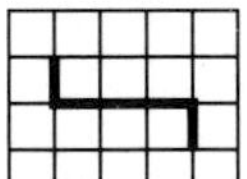

602 Forest Green-med. (border in center panel)

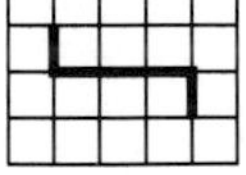

600 Forest Green-vy.dk. (border in side panels)

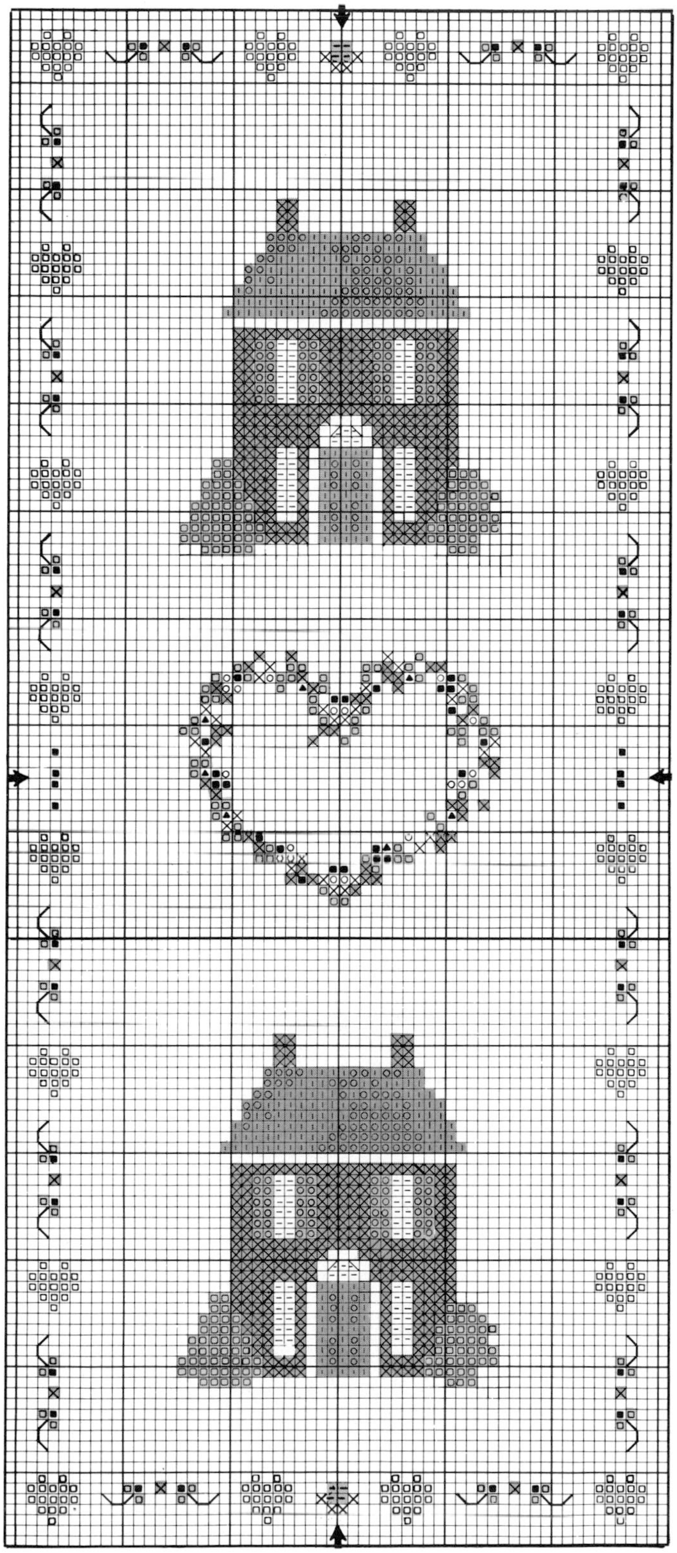

Center Panel
Stitch Count: 58 x 140

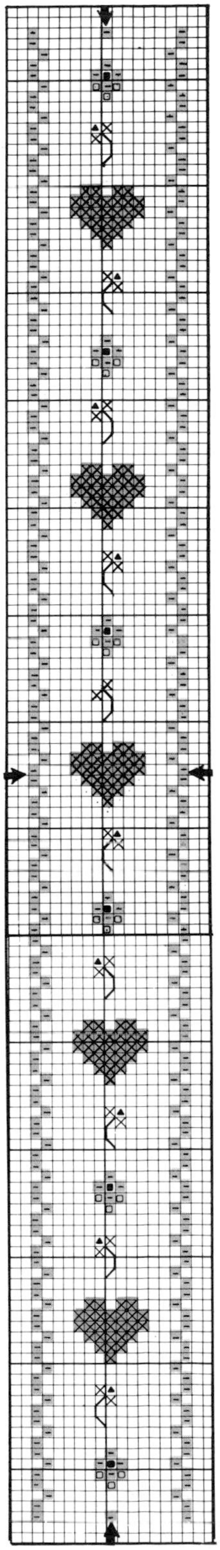

Side Panel
Stitch Count: 15 x 140

Piney Scents

Stitched on amaretto Murano 30 over 2 threads, the finished design size for the horse is 2½" x 2". The fabric was cut 16" x 13". Repeat each border motif two times above and two times below graphed section. Heavy lines indicate repeats.

FABRICS	DESIGN SIZES
Aida 11	3½" x 2¾"
Aida 14	2¾" x 2⅛"
Aida 18	2⅛" x 1⅝"
Hardanger 22	1¾" x 1⅜"

Anchor		DMC (used for sample)	
	Step 1: Cross-stitch (2 strands)		
13	△	347	Salmon-vy. dk.
921	X	931	Antique Blue-med.
266	−	471	Avocado Green-vy. lt.
363	•	436	Tan
370	X	434	Brown-lt.
352	●	300	Mahogany-vy. dk.
	Step 2: Backstitch (1 strand)		
236		3799	Pewter Gray-vy. dk.

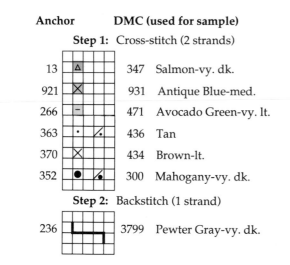

MATERIALS

Completed cross-stitch design on amaretto Murano 30; matching thread
⅜ yard of muslin
3½ yards of 1/16"-wide blue flat rayon braid
3-4 cups of chopped green pine needles
One sharp large-eyed needle
Four 1"-long pine cones
Glue gun and glue

DIRECTIONS

1. With horse centered horizontally and borders aligned vertically with short edges, trim design piece to measure 15" x 12¼". From muslin cut one 14" x 11" piece for inner pouch. Cut four equal lengths from braid.

2. To make inner pouch, fold muslin with right sides facing and raw edges aligned to measure 14" x 5½". Stitch all edges, leaving an opening. Turn. Fill pouch with pine needles; stitch opening closed.

3. To make pillow, fold design piece to measure 15" x 6⅛"; stitch the long edge. Turn. Insert pouch. Fold ends ½" to wrong side. Thread needle with two lengths of braid and sew ¼" running stitch through each end near fold. Gather and tie braids in a bow. Glue one pine cone to each ribbon tail (see photo).

Stitch Count: 38 x 30

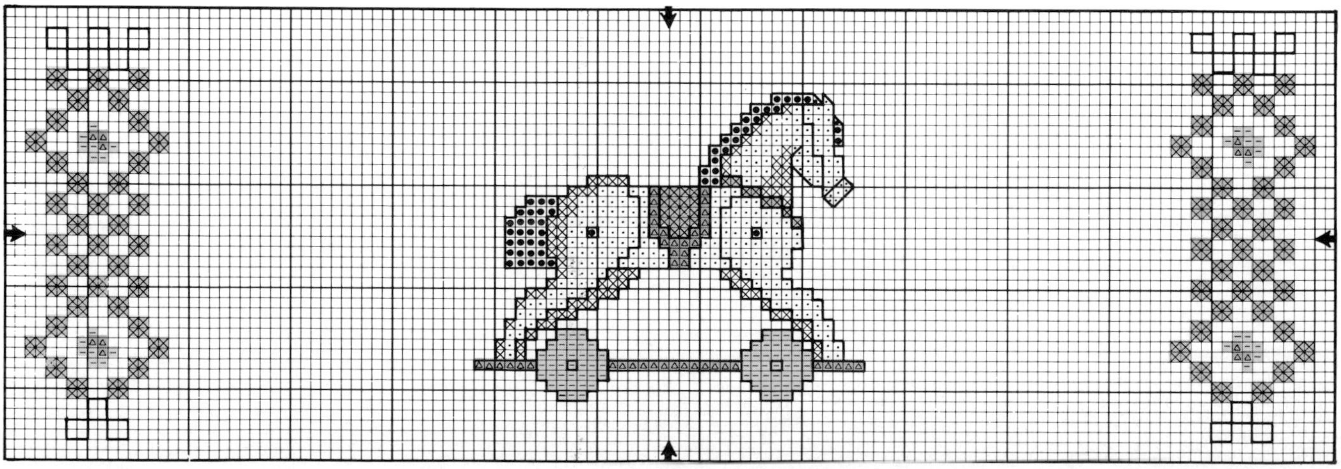

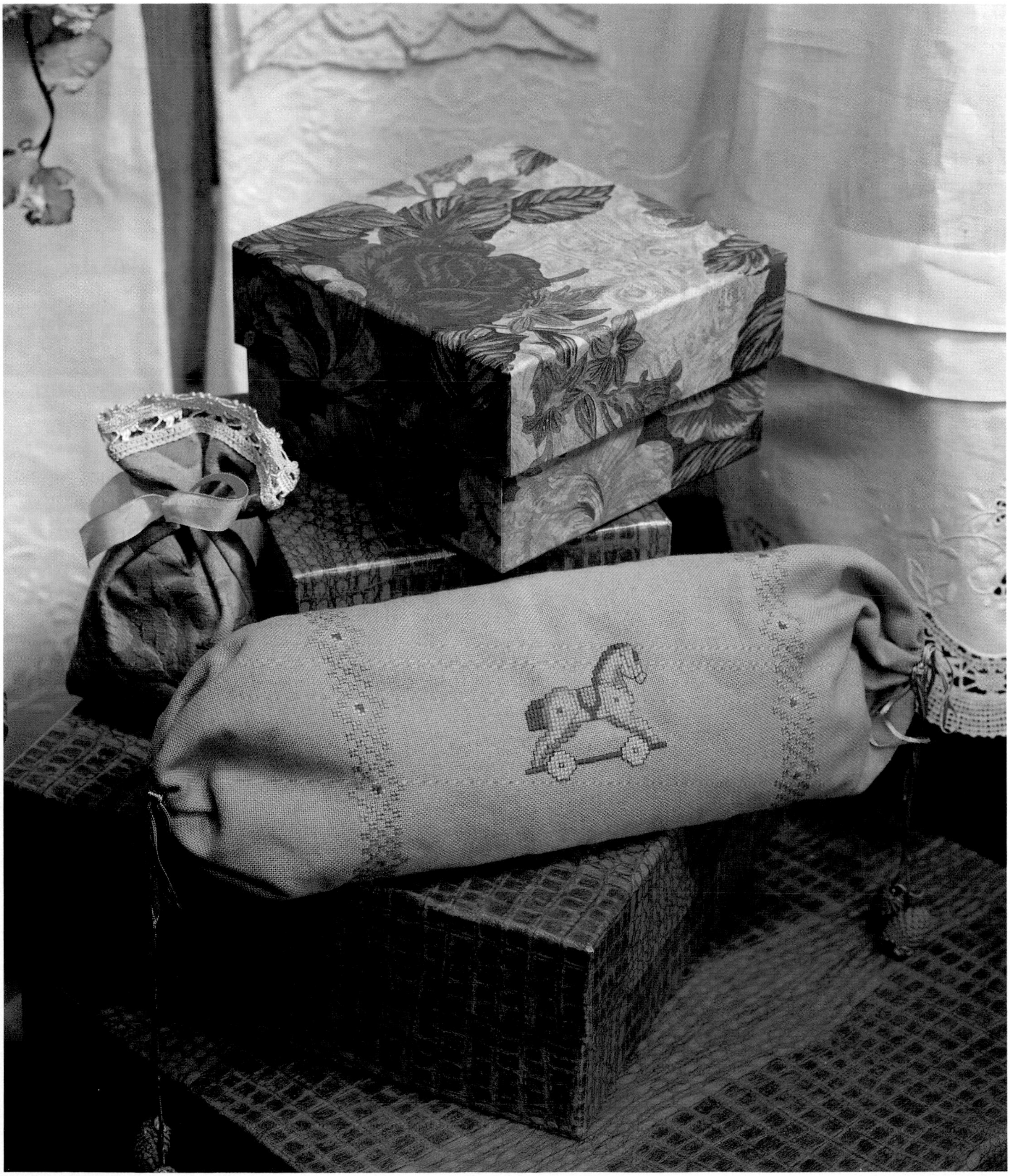

Everything says that fall is in the air—the harvest-ready foods, the falling leaves, the short, sunny days. It is time to slow down and savor the bounty of wonder and warmth, of home and hearth.

Stitch Count: 142 x 116

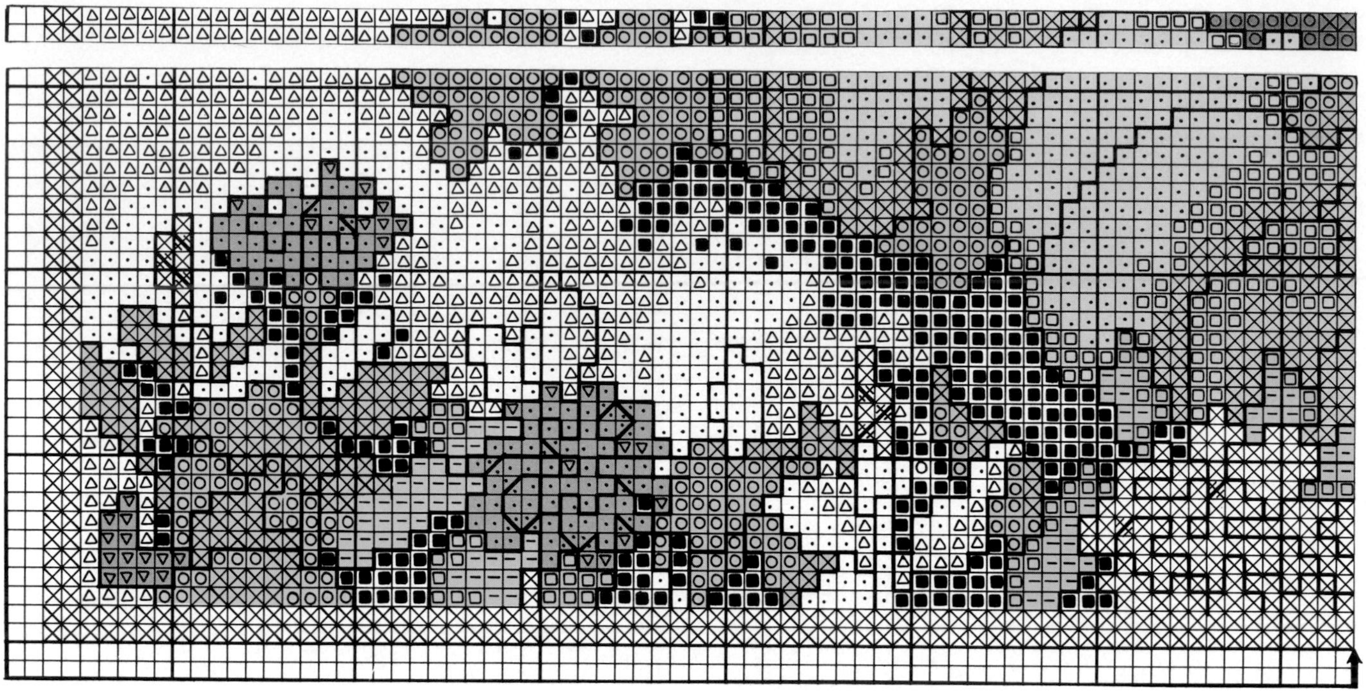

Pumpkins on the Wall

Stitched on ivory Aida 14 over 1 thread, the finished design size is 10⅛" x 8¼". The fabric was cut 17" x 15".

FABRICS	DESIGN SIZES
Aida 11	12⅞" x 10½"
Aida 18	7⅞" x 6½"
Hardanger 22	6½" x 5¼"

Anchor **DMC (used for sample)**

Step 1: Cross-stitch (2 strands)

Anchor	Symbol	DMC	Color
1	%.		White
892	S	3770	Peach Pecan-vy. lt.
886	–	677	Old Gold-vy. lt.
891	O	676	Old Gold-lt.
890	X	729	Old Gold-med.
887	●	372	Mustard-lt.
347	•	402	Mahogany-vy. lt.
324	□	922	Copper-lt.
349	X	921	Copper
868	E	3779	Terra Cotta-vy. lt.
10	•	3712	Salmon-med.
894	O	223	Shell Pink-med.
13	▽	347	Salmon-vy. dk.
20	X	498	Christmas Red-dk.

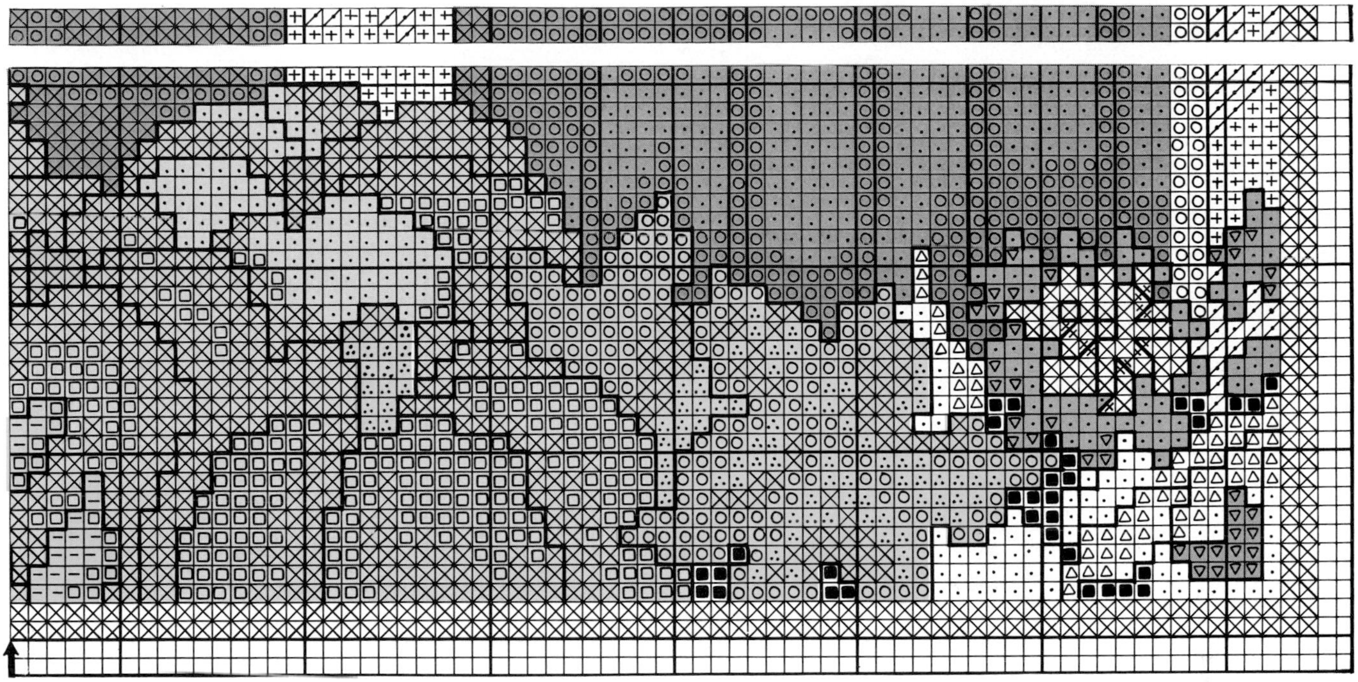

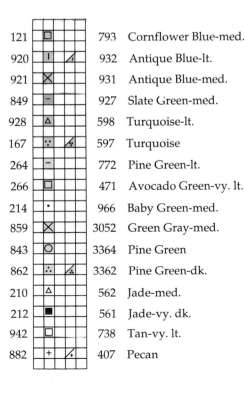

Anchor	Symbol	DMC	Color
121	□	793	Cornflower Blue-med.
920	I	932	Antique Blue-lt.
921	×	931	Antique Blue-med.
849	−	927	Slate Green-med.
928	△	598	Turquoise-lt.
167	∵	597	Turquoise
264	−	772	Pine Green-lt.
266	□	471	Avocado Green-vy. lt.
214	•	966	Baby Green-med.
859	×	3052	Green Gray-med.
843	○	3364	Pine Green
862	∴	3362	Pine Green-dk.
210	△	562	Jade-med.
212	■	561	Jade-vy. dk.
942	□	738	Tan-vy. lt.
882	+	407	Pecan
914	/	3064	Pecan-lt.
936	∵	3772	Pecan-med.
376	U	842	Beige Brown-vy. lt.
379	◘	840	Beige Brown-med.
380	▲	839	Beige Brown-dk.
900	○	648	Beaver Gray-lt.
8581	×	646	Beaver Gray-dk.
397	•	762	Pearl Gray-vy. lt.
236	∴	3799	Pewter Gray-vy. dk.

Step 2: Backstitch (1 strand)

Anchor	DMC	Color
13	347	Salmon-vy. dk. (in doll's dress)
236	3799	Pewter Gray-vy. dk. (all else)

Step 3: French knot (1 strand)

Anchor	DMC	Color
236	3799	Pewter Gray-vy. dk.

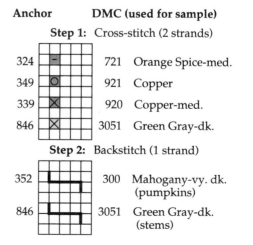

The Scents of Fall

Stitched on cream Belfast Linen 32 over 2 threads, the finished design size is 6" x 1½". The fabric was cut 10" x 8".

FABRICS	**DESIGN SIZES**
Aida 11	8⅞" x 2⅛"
Aida 14	6⅞" x 1⅝"
Aida 18	5⅜" x 1¼"
Hardanger 22	4⅜" x 1"

Anchor **DMC (used for sample)**

Step 1: Cross-stitch (2 strands)

Anchor	Symbol	DMC	Color
324	-	721	Orange Spice-med.
349	O	921	Copper
339	X (shaded)	920	Copper-med.
846	X	3051	Green Gray-dk.

Step 2: Backstitch (1 strand)

Anchor	DMC	Color
352	300	Mahogany-vy. dk. (pumpkins)
846	3051	Green Gray-dk. (stems)

MATERIALS

Completed cross-stitch design on cream Belfast Linen 32
½ yard of pine green paisley chintz; matching thread
¼ yard of pine green chintz
One 8½" x 8" piece each of navy, tan, and rust chintzes
1¾ yards of ½"-wide dark green satin ribbon
1¼ yards each of ⅛"-wide rust and navy blue satin ribbons; matching threads
3½ yards of medium cording
Stuffing
Three cups of potpourri (see General Instructions)

DIRECTIONS

1. Trim design piece to measure 8½" x 6" with design centered horizontally and top of stitching 1" from top edge of fabric. From paisley chintz, cut two 15" x 12" pieces for pillow front and back and one 8½" x 6" piece for pocket lining. Cut two 8½" lengths from each color of ribbon. From pine green chintz, cut 1½"-wide bias strips, piecing as needed to equal 126". Make 87" of corded piping and 39" of corded tubing (see General Instructions).

2. To make pocket, slipstitch one 8½" rust ribbon 1" from bottom edge of design piece. Stitch remaining 8½" ribbons ⅛" apart in the following order: navy blue, dark green, rust, dark green, and navy blue (see photo). Cut a 30" length of piping and stitch to right side of design piece with raw edges aligned. Stitch lining to design piece with right sides facing, leaving an opening. Turn. Slipstitch the opening closed.

To attach pocket to pillow front, place pocket 1¾" from one long edge of one 15" paisley piece and center horizontally (see photo). Stitch-in-the-ditch between piping and design piece along sides and bottom of pocket.

3. Stitch remaining piping to right side of pillow front with raw edges aligned. Stitch pillow front to back with right sides facing, leaving an opening. Turn. Stuff firmly. Slipstitch opening closed. Tie remaining ribbons in a bow and tack on right side of pocket (see photo).

4. To make potpourri bags, fold each 8½" x 8" chintz piece with right sides facing to measure 4¼" x 8". Stitch the long edge and one short edge. Clip corners. Turn. Sew a ¼" hem on remaining raw edge. Fill bags ¾ full with potpourri. From corded tubing, cut three 13" lengths; knot ends. Tie 1½" from top of each bag and place in pillow pocket (see photo).

Stitch Count: 97 x 23

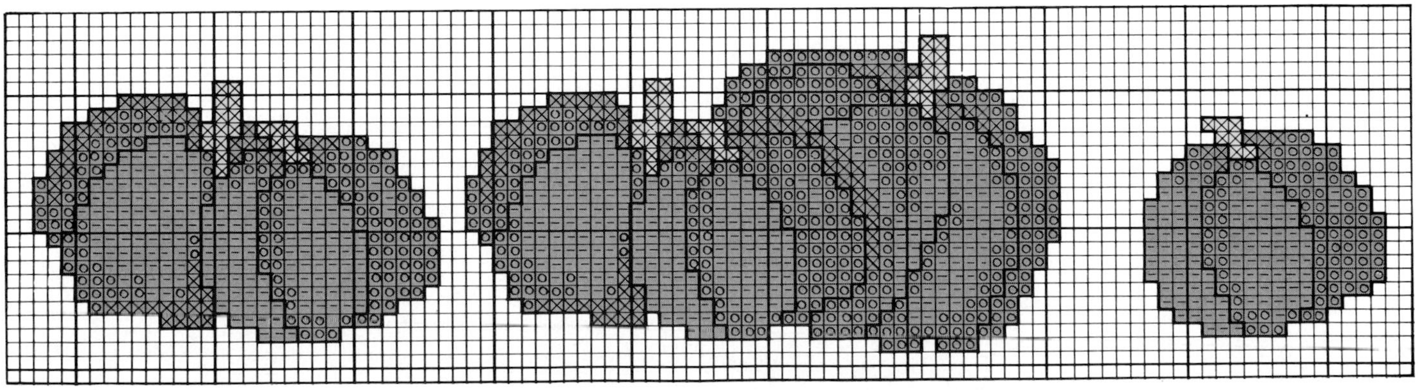

Christmas is . . . songs of joy and good cheer, ice skating on pristine lakes, the smell of fresh pine, the joy of a child opening a most-wanted gift, and the quivering brightness of an Advent candle's glow as we count these precious days.

MERRY
CHRISTMAS

Christmas Scenes

Stitched on cream Belfast Linen 32 over 2 threads, the finished design size is 12⅞" x 10⅜". The fabric was cut 19" x 17".

FABRICS	DESIGN SIZES
Aida 11	18¾" x 15⅛"
Aida 14	14¾" x 11⅞"
Aida 18	11½" x 9¼"
Hardanger 22	9⅜" x 7½"

Step 1: Cross-stitch (2 strands)

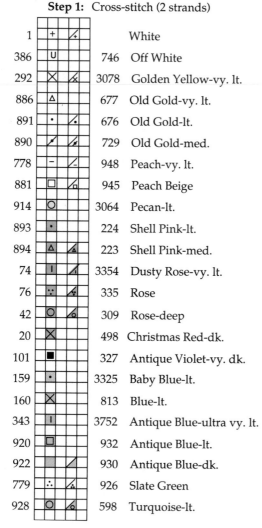

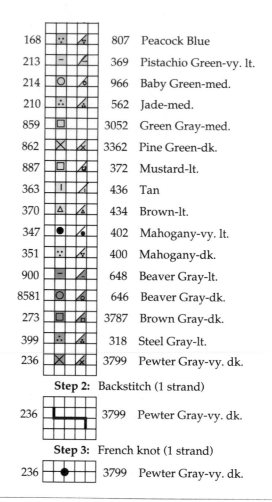

Anchor	**DMC (used for sample)**	
1		White
386	746	Off White
292	3078	Golden Yellow-vy. lt.
886	677	Old Gold-vy. lt.
891	676	Old Gold-lt.
890	729	Old Gold-med.
778	948	Peach-vy. lt.
881	945	Peach Beige
914	3064	Pecan-lt.
893	224	Shell Pink-lt.
894	223	Shell Pink-med.
74	3354	Dusty Rose-vy. lt.
76	335	Rose
42	309	Rose-deep
20	498	Christmas Red-dk.
101	327	Antique Violet-vy. dk.
159	3325	Baby Blue-lt.
160	813	Blue-lt.
343	3752	Antique Blue-ultra vy. lt.
920	932	Antique Blue-lt.
922	930	Antique Blue-dk.
779	926	Slate Green
928	598	Turquoise-lt.
168	807	Peacock Blue
213	369	Pistachio Green-vy. lt.
214	966	Baby Green-med.
210	562	Jade-med.
859	3052	Green Gray-med.
862	3362	Pine Green-dk.
887	372	Mustard-lt.
363	436	Tan
370	434	Brown-lt.
347	402	Mahogany-vy. lt.
351	400	Mahogany-dk.
900	648	Beaver Gray-lt.
8581	646	Beaver Gray-dk.
273	3787	Brown Gray-dk.
399	318	Steel Gray-lt.
236	3799	Pewter Gray-vy. dk.

Step 2: Backstitch (1 strand)

236	3799	Pewter Gray-vy. dk.

Step 3: French knot (1 strand)

236	3799	Pewter Gray-vy. dk.

Stitch Count: 206 x 166

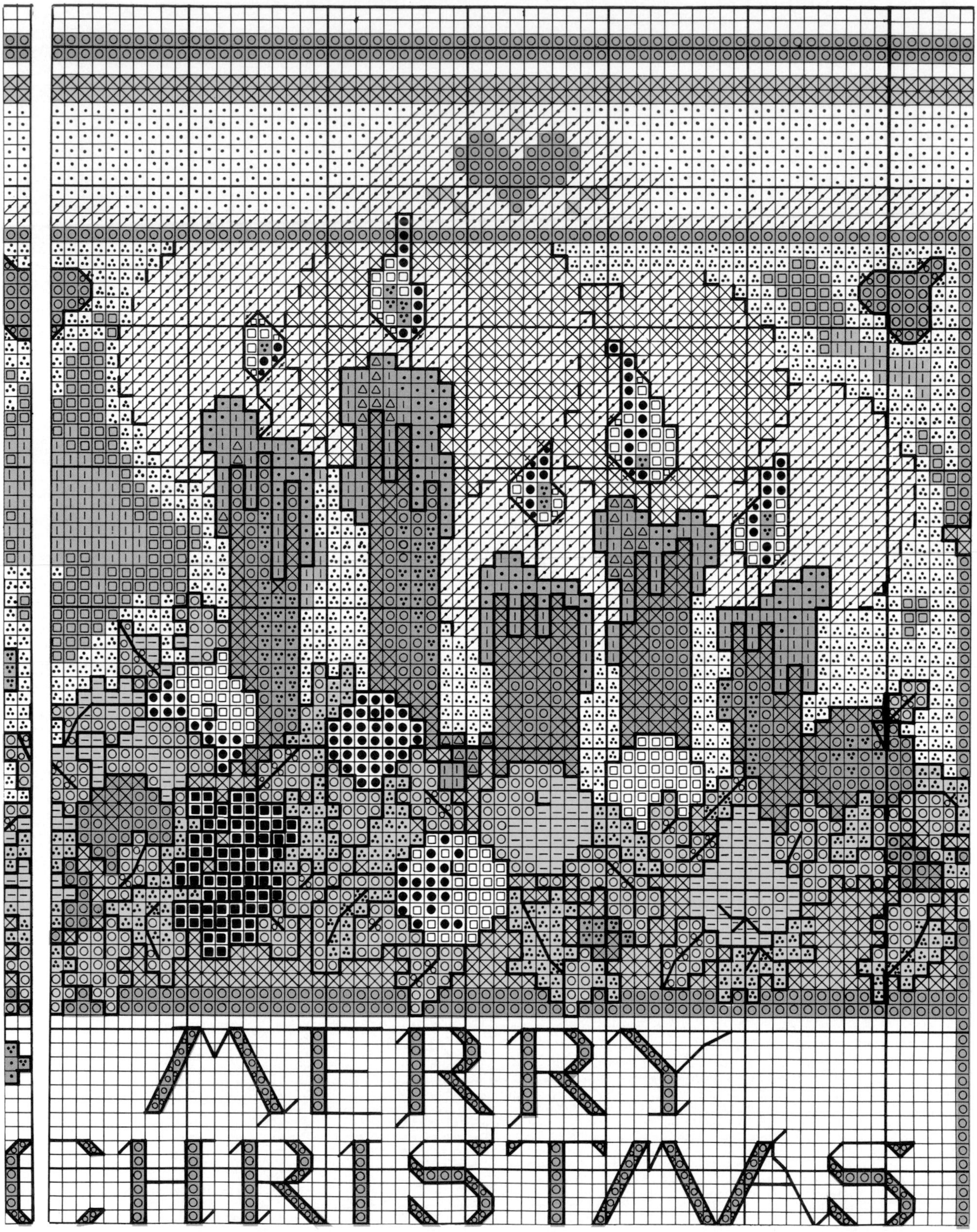
MERRY
CHRISTMAS

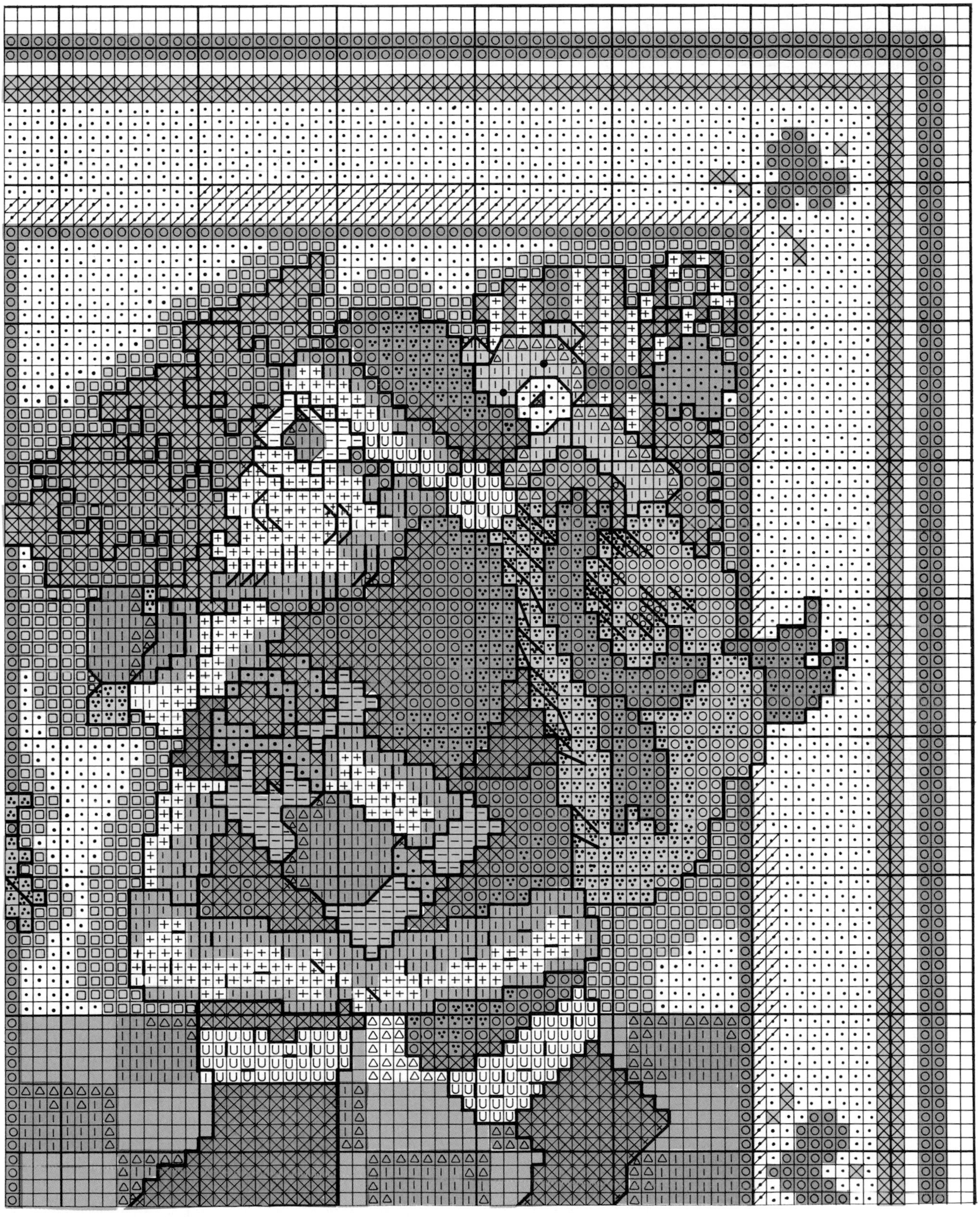

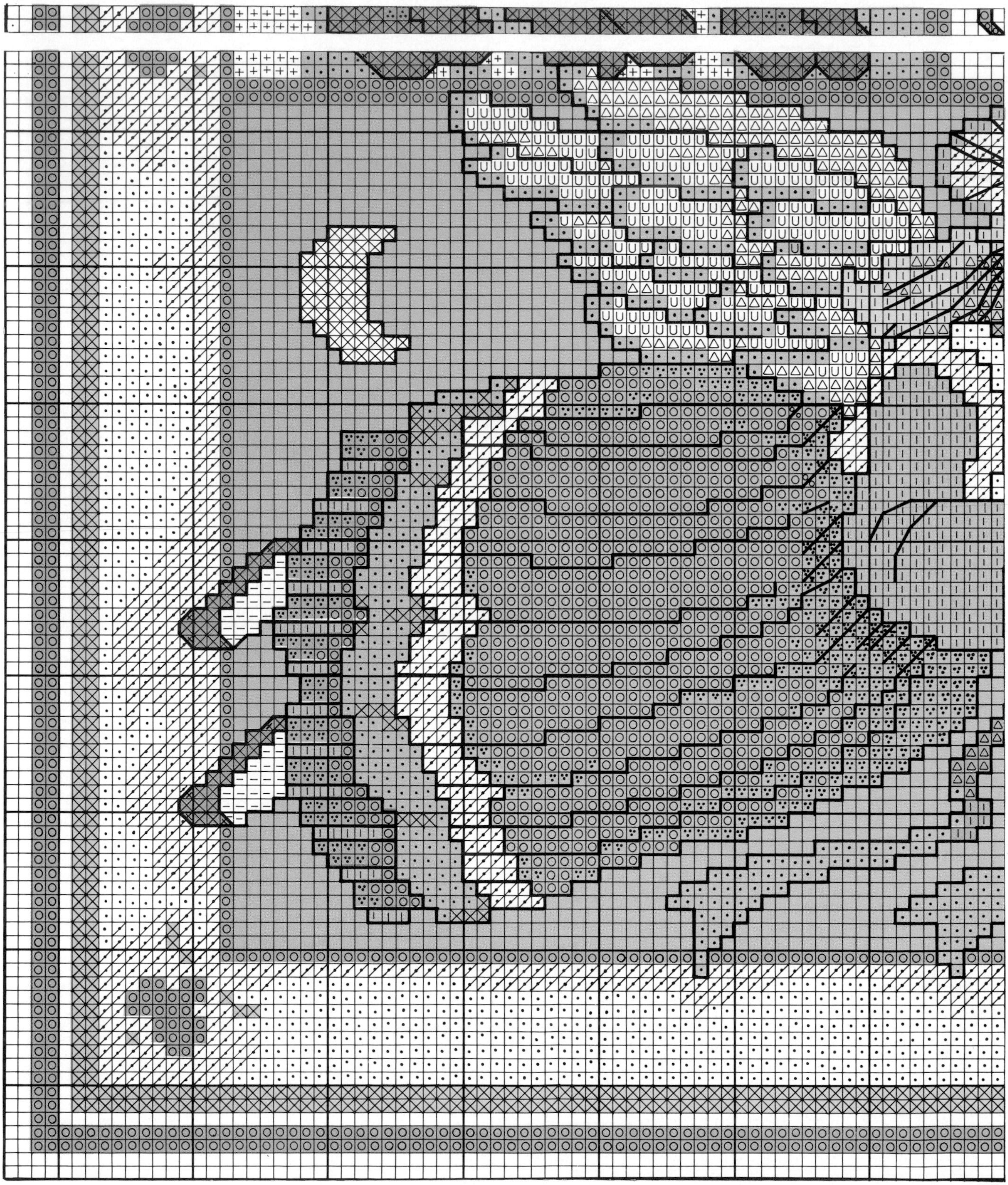

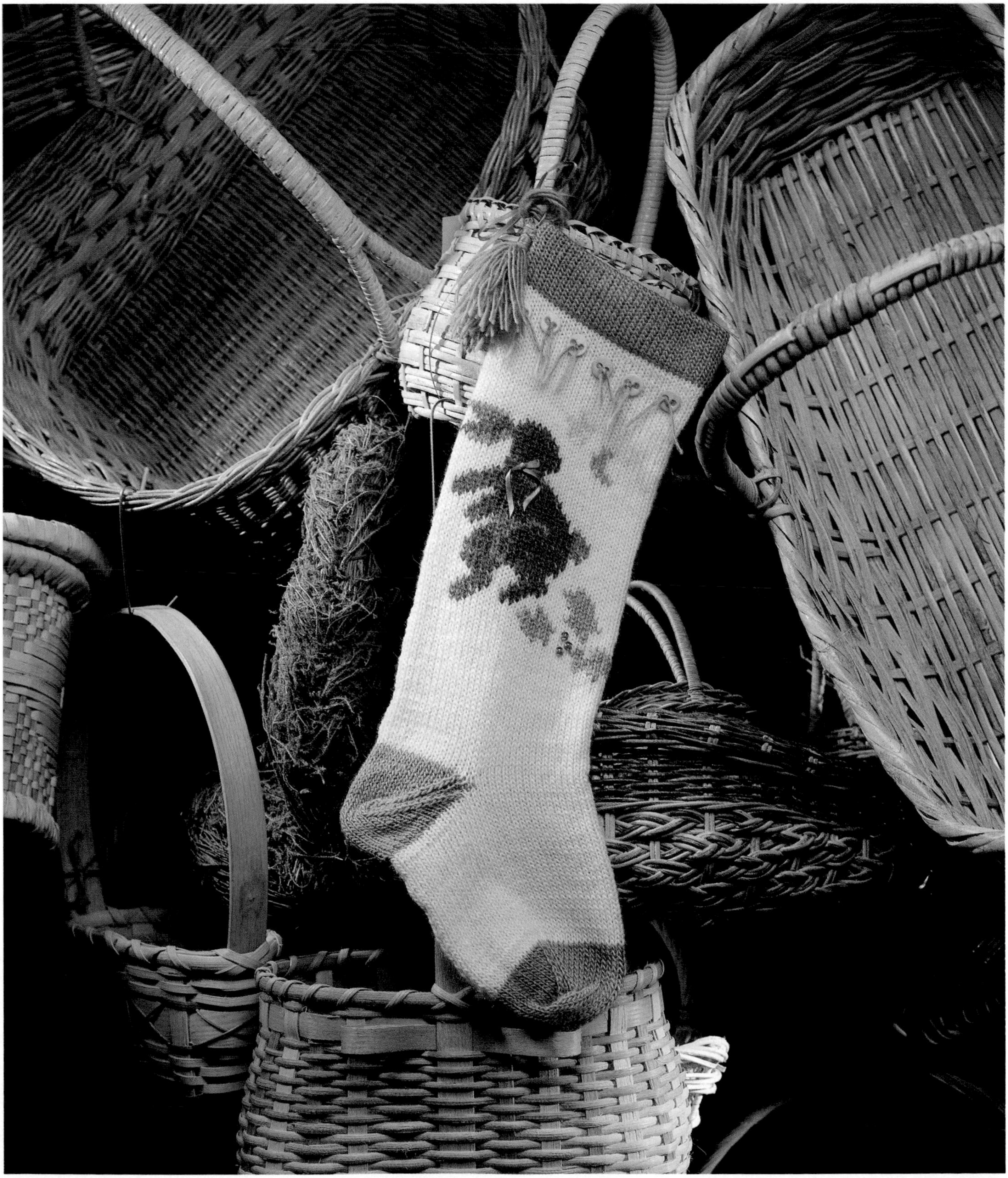

Some Bunny Loves You

MATERIALS
Yarn description: Sportweight, Green (A), Natural (B); Persian yarns (see code for colors)
Yarn pictured: Filatura Di Crosa Sympathie,* 50-gr., 136 m skeins, 1 skein Willow Green (A), 2 skeins Natural #700 (B); Paternayan Persian Yarns* (see code for colors)
Tools: One pair 14"-long knitting needles, Size 3; tapestry needle No. 18; 3"-4" stitch holders
1¼ yards of ⅛"-wide mauve satin ribbon
Six ½"-wide cream buttons
Three amethyst pebble beads*
One 5" x 5" piece of cardboard
*see Suppliers

GAUGE
11 sts = 2"
9 rows = 1"

DIRECTIONS
Beginning at top of stocking, with A, cast on 68 sts. Knit one row, purl one row in stockinette st for 3"—approximately 28 rows. Leave a 3" end, cut yarn. With B, cont to work in stockinette st until piece measures 14"—approximately 100 rows. Do not fasten off.

Preparation for heel section: With A, knit across 17 sts, (this yarn will be removed later to free these 17 sts to be worked for heel section), leave a 3" end of yarn, cut yarn, turn, slip these 17 sts back onto needle holding rem sts. Pick up B, knot across to last 17 sts, drop B. With A, knit rem 17 sts, leave a 3" end of yarn, cut yarn, turn, slip these 17 sts back onto free needle. Pick up B, knit across these 17 sts, cont with B, work 36 rows of stockinette st across all 68 sts, cut yarn.

Toe: First side section: work short rows: With A, P-17, place rem st on holder, turn, K-1, sl 1, K-1, PSSO, K rem 14 sts, turn, P across, turn, K-1, sl 1, K-1, PSSO, K rem 13 sts, turn, P across, turn, K-1, sl 1, K-1, PSSO, K-12, turn, P across, turn, K-1, sl 1, K-1, PSSO, K-11, turn, P across, turn, K-1, sl 1, K-1, PSSO, K-10, turn, P across, turn, K-1, sl 1, K-1, PSSO, K-9, turn, P across, turn, K-1, sl 1, K-1, PSSO, K-8, turn, P across, turn, K-1, sl 1, K-1, PSSO, K-7, turn, P across - 9 sts. Place rem 9 sts on holder. Leave an 18" end of yarn, cut yarn.

Center section: Slip center 34 sts to needle, join A, P across, turn.

Row 1: K-1, sl 1, K-1, PSSO, K-28, K-2 tog, K-1.
Row 2: P-34.
Row 3: K-1, sl 1, K-1, PSSO, K-26, K-2 tog, K-1.
Row 4: P-32
Row 5: K-1, sl 1, K-1, PSSO, K-24, K-2 tog, K-1.

Cont in this same manner until there are 14 sts bet dec sts. P-18. Leave an 18" end of yarn, cut yarn.

Second side section: Sl rem 17 sts from holder to needle, join A.

Row 1: P-17.
Row 2: K-14, K-2 tog, K-1.
Row 3: P-16
Row 4: K-13, K-2 tog, K-1.

Cont in this same manner until 9 sts rem. Leave an 18" end of yarn, cut yarn. Place 9 sts from first holder and 9 sts from needle on a needle with dec areas at each end. Place center 18 sts on other needle, weave sts tog for toe. Weave all toe seams tog.

Heel: Remove green yarn from heel area of one side of stocking. Place 17 live sts from foot edge onto a holder, and the 17 lives sts from ankle edge onto the needle, beg with a purl. Join A, work same as first side section of toe. Slip 17 sts from holder, work same as second side section of toe, weave 9 sts tog. Remove green yarn from other heel area, work same as other heel sections, reverse shaping. Weave 9 sts tog.

Duplicate stitch: Stitch on knitted stocking. The finished design size is 5½" x 9½". Following the graph, locate "V" to be covered by first stitch and come up from behind at base of "V." Insert needle through upper right point of "V," then through upper left point (Diagrams 1-3).

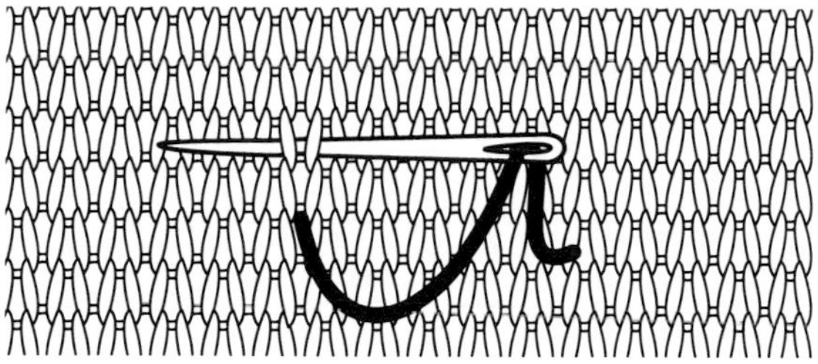

Diagram 1

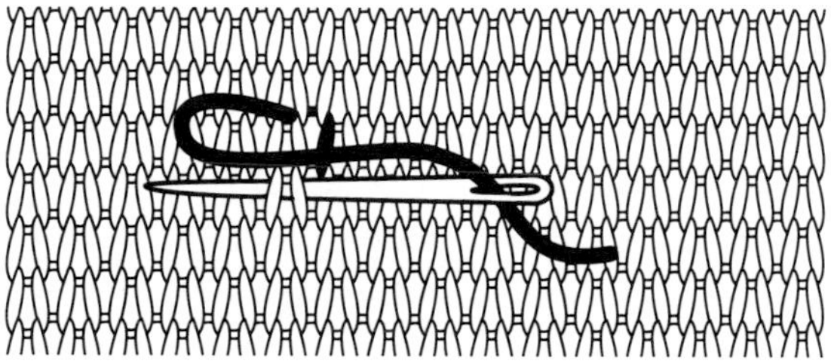

Diagram 2

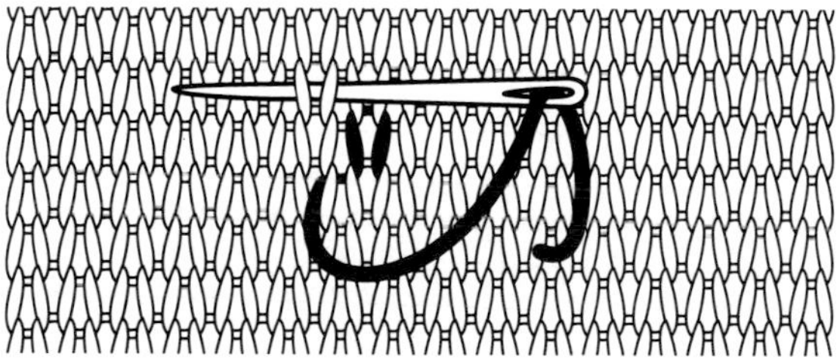

Diagram 3

Paternayan Persian Yarn (used for sample)

Step 1: Duplicate stitch

Symbol	No.	Color
–	727	Autumn Yellow-vy. lt.
∴	864	Copper-lt.
○	663	Pine Green-med.
○	434	Chocolate Brown
☒	432	Chocolate Brown-dk.

Step 2: Attach Pebble bead

Symbol	No.	Color
●	05202	Amethyst

Step 3: Ribbon placement: Tie one 8" piece of ribbon in a bow and attach to bunny. (■)

Finishing: Weave all heel seams tog. Weave back seam of stocking tog. To form the hem, at top fold green section in half to inside of stocking and whipstitch in place.

To make tassel, cut one 8" and one 5" piece of A. Set aside. Wind A around cardboard 30 times. Using 5" piece of yarn, knot at top to secure. Cut threads at opposite end (Diagram 4).

Diagram 4

Using 8" piece of yarn, lay a narrow loop of yarn flat on tassel, looped end down and extending below area to be wrapped (Diagram 5).

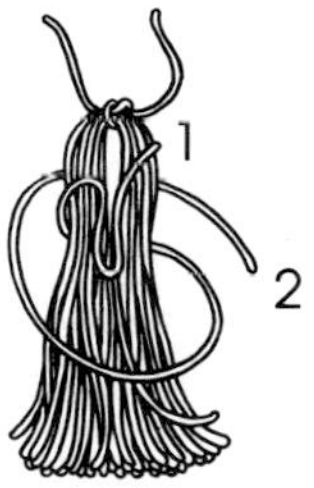

Diagram 5

Wrap yarn over two strands that form the loop to secure. Then insert 2 through loop (Diagram 6).

Diagram 6

Pull up on 1 to secure loop and thread inside neck (Diagram 7). Cut off ends.

Diagram 7

To form loop for hanging, cut six 6" strands of A. Handling strands as one unit, thread through loop at top of tassel. Knot ends together. Move knot to top of tassel; trim ends. Hide knot by wrapping remaining ribbon around tassel, leaving long tails. Tack tassel to top of stocking (see photo).

Using A, tie buttons to stocking front at ½" intervals, leaving 2"-long yarn tails (see photo).

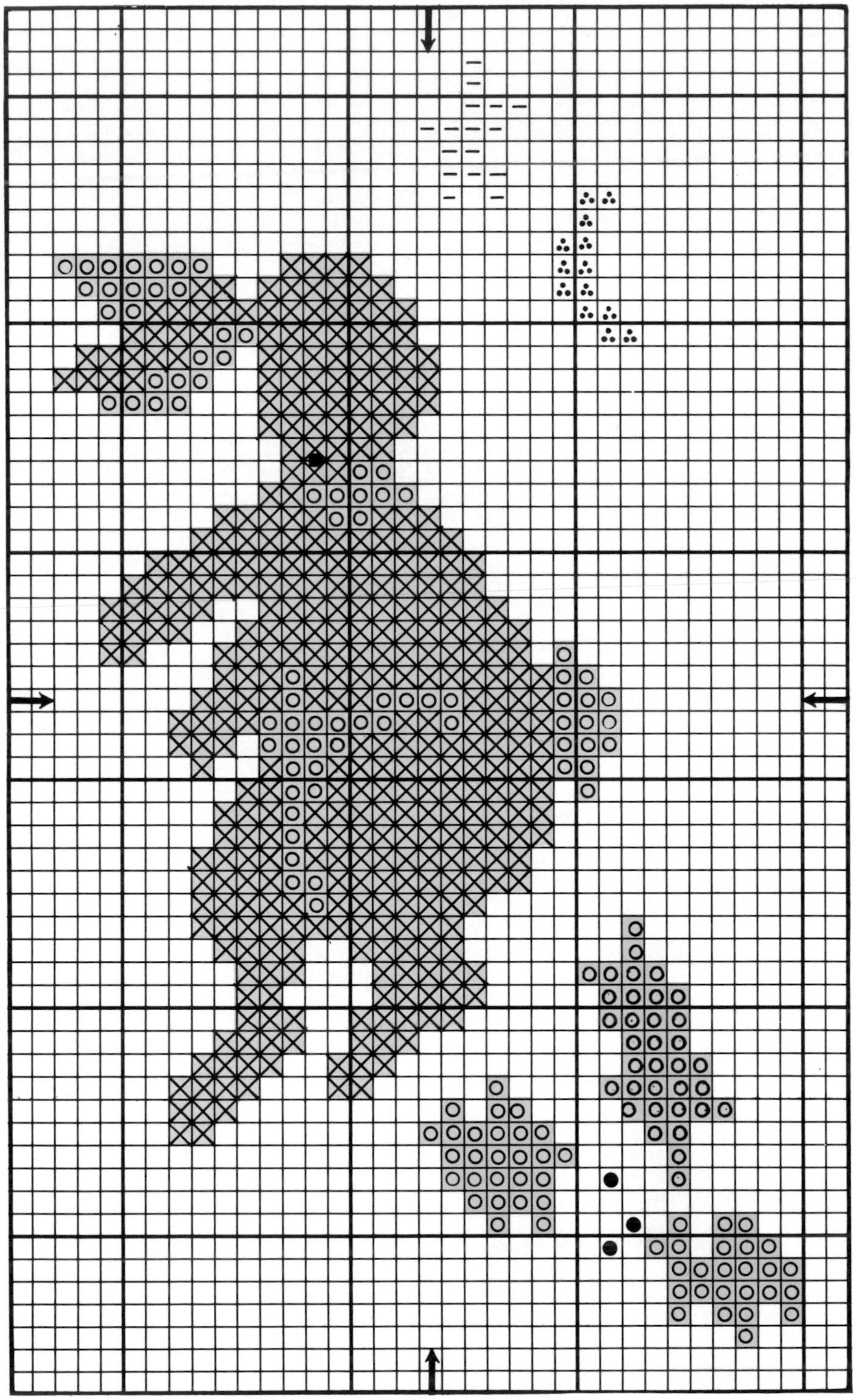

Stitch Count: 33 x 97

Tiny Trimmings

Stitched on white Belfast Linen 32 over 2 threads, the finished design sizes are: Santa, 2⅛" x 2¼"; rocking horse, 2" x 1⅞"; candles, 2¼" x 2¼"; and angel, 2" x 1¾". The fabric for each stocking was cut 8" x 5".

FABRICS	DESIGN SIZES Santa	DESIGN SIZES Rocking Horse
Aida 11	3⅛" x 3⅛"	3" x 2¾"
Aida 14	2⅜" x 2½"	2⅜" x 2⅛"
Aida 18	1⅞" x 2"	1⅞" x 1⅝"
Hardanger 22	1½" x 1⅝"	1½" x 1⅜"

FABRICS	DESIGN SIZES Candles	DESIGN SIZES Angel
Aida 11	3⅛" x 3⅜"	3" x 2½"
Aida 14	2½" x 2⅝"	2⅜" x 2"
Aida 18	2" x 2"	1⅞" x 1½"
Hardanger 22	1⅝" x 1⅝"	1½" x 1¼"

Anchor **DMC (used for sample)**

Step 1: Cross-stitch (2 strands)

Anchor	DMC	Color
1		White
386	746	Off White
292	3078	Golden Yellow-vy. lt.
891	676	Old Gold-lt.
892	225	Shell Pink-vy. lt.
10	3712	Salmon-med.
74	3354	Dusty Rose-vy. lt.
76	335	Rose
42	309	Rose-deep
22	816	Garnet
343	3752	Antique Blue-ultra vy. lt.
167	597	Turquoise
168	807	Peacock Blue
161	826	Blue-med.
264	772	Pine Green-lt.
214	966	Baby Green-med.
843	3364	Pine Green
862	3362	Pine Green-dk.
210	562	Jade-med.
212	561	Jade-vy. dk.
347	402	Mahogany-vy. lt.
352	300	Mahogany-vy. dk.
900	648	Beaver Gray-lt.
236	3799	Pewter Gray-vy. dk.
403	310	Black

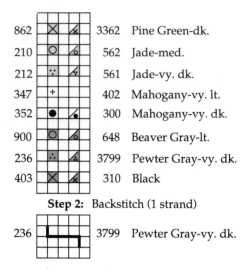

Step 2: Backstitch (1 strand)

Anchor	DMC	Color
236	3799	Pewter Gray-vy. dk.

MATERIALS for one stocking

Completed cross-stitch design on white Belfast Linen 32; matching thread
Scrap of unstitched white Belfast Linen 32
Scrap of coordinating satin
One 6" square of polyester fleece
One 16" x 7" piece of fusible knit interfacing
4" of ⅛"-wide ribbon
10" of small cording
1¼ yards of ⅜"-wide white and gold braid

DIRECTIONS

1. Place cuff pattern over design piece, centered horizontally and with point ¾" below stitching; cut.

2. From both unstitched linen and fleece cut two stockings. Cut one cuff from interfacing. From satin, cut

Stitch Count: 33 x 28

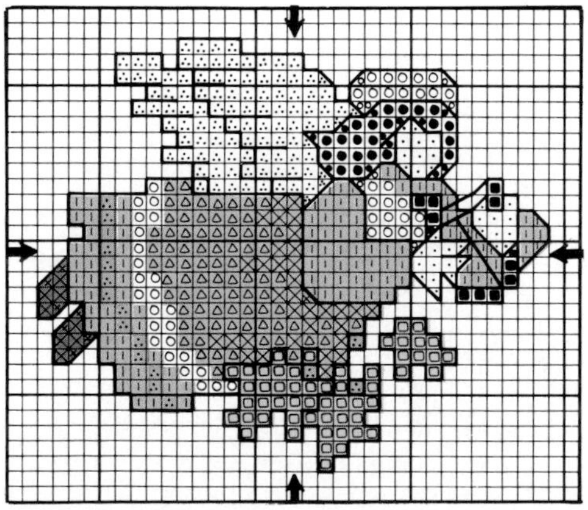

1¼"-wide bias strips to equal 10". Make 10" of corded piping.

3. Baste one fleece stocking to wrong side of each linen stocking. Then stitch stockings together with right sides facing, leaving top edge open. Trim fleece from seam allowances. Clip curves; turn.

4. Fuse interfacing cuff to wrong side of design piece following manufacturer's instructions. Fold under ¼" on top and back edges of cuff (see pattern); zigzag folded edges through all layers. Stitch corded piping on seam allowance of diagonal edges, right sides facing and raw edges aligned. Fold the seam to wrong side of cuff; press.

Stitch Count: 35 x 37

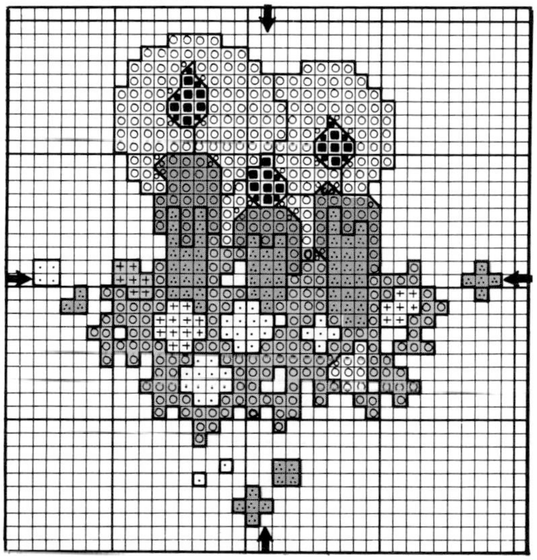

Stitch Count: 34 x 35

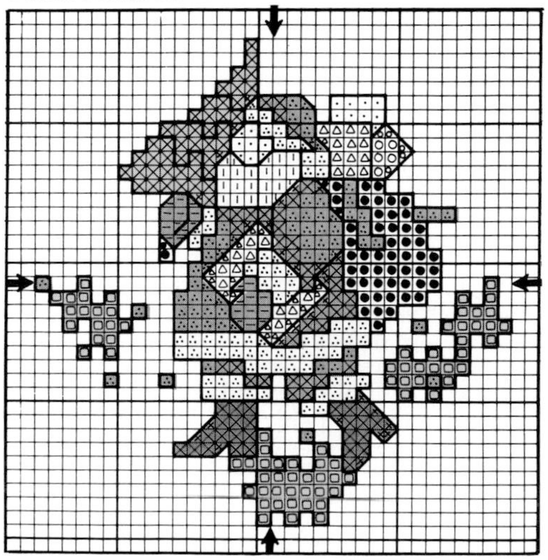

5. Place cuff with top 1¼" above top edge of stocking front, centering design horizontally. Wrap cuff to back of stocking, overlapping in back and adjusting to fit; tack. Fold top of cuff inside stocking. Blindstitch inside edge of cuff to seam allowance on top edge of stocking. If desired, fold ribbon to form a 2" hanger loop and tack ends to inside of stocking near right seam. To make three more stockings, repeat Steps 1 through 5. String stockings on braid (see photo).

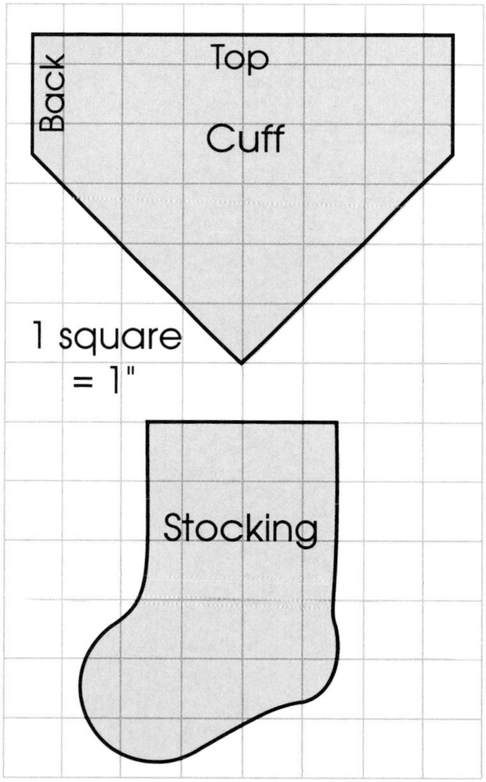

Stitch Count: 33 x 30

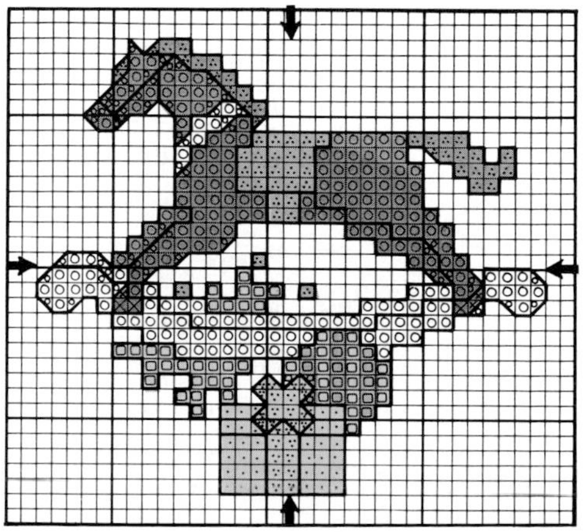

These cats are out of the bag, ready to march right into your heart. Their feline ways are adapted to the events of the year, ready to accompany you on every occasion. You'll not want to pussyfoot around—making them is half the fun!

New Year's Eve Gala

Sir Alistair Cat

Stitched on pewter Murano 30 over 2 threads, the finished design size is 2⅜" x ¾". The fabric was cut 9" x 3". Repeat motif until stitching equals 6½" inches. Heavy lines indicate repeats.

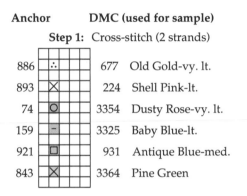

Anchor		DMC (used for sample)	
	Step 1:	Cross-stitch (2 strands)	
886	∴	677	Old Gold-vy. lt.
893	X	224	Shell Pink-lt.
74	O	3354	Dusty Rose-vy. lt.
159	-	3325	Baby Blue-lt.
921	□	931	Antique Blue-med.
843	X	3364	Pine Green

MATERIALS

Cat body and ceramic head (see Suppliers)
Completed cross-stitch design on pewter Murano 30
⅛ yard of dark blue faux suede fabric; matching thread
Scrap of dark blue polyester lining fabric
⅛ yard of white fabric with ¼"-wide pintucks
Scrap of light blue satin
⅜ yard of ¼"-wide light blue trim
Four small snap sets
Two hook-and-eye sets

DIRECTIONS

1. Trim design piece to measure 7¼" x 1½", centering design. From suede, cut four pants, two jacket fronts, one jacket back, two sleeves, one jacket collar and one ⅜" x 7" piece for bow tie. From lining fabric, cut two jacket fronts, two sleeves, one jacket back and one collar. From white fabric, cut one shirt front, two shirt backs, two shirt sleeves and one shirt collar. From satin, cut one 7¼" x 1⅜" piece and two 7¼" x ⅝" pieces for cummerbund.

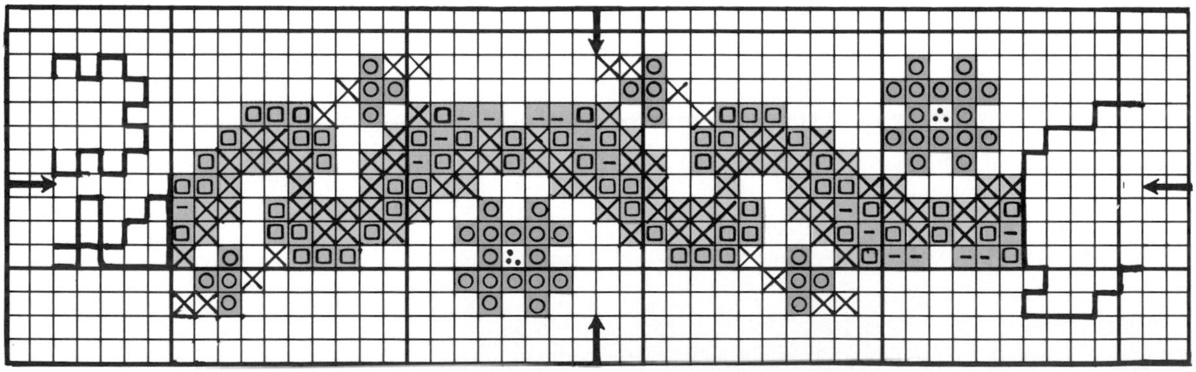

Stitch Count: 36 x 11

2. To make shirt, stitch shirt front to shirt backs at shoulders with right sides facing. Fold collar with right sides facing and long edges aligned. Stitch ends; turn. Then sew to neck edge with right sides facing.

Sew ¼" hem on bottom edges of both sleeves. Stitch one sleeve cap to armhole with right sides facing. Stitch shirt side seam, then sleeve seam with right sides facing. Repeat for other sleeve. Fold ¼" to wrong side on center backs; topstitch. Sew three snap sets to back edges of shirt. Sew ¼" hem on bottom of shirt.

3. To make bow tie, tie suede in bow, placing ends to back. Cut "V" in each end. Center and tack below collar on shirt front (see photo).

4. To make jacket, stitch suede and lining fabric collars along outer edge (see pattern) with right sides facing. Clip curves. Turn. Slipstitch trim to suede side, ⅛" from outer edge. Stitch suede jacket fronts to jacket back at shoulders with right sides facing. Repeat with lining pieces. Matching centers, place lining side of collar over right side of suede jacket at neck; baste. With right sides of jacket and lining facing, match shoulder seams and stitch bottoms of jacket fronts, center front and neck edge, securing collar in seam. Clip curves. Turn. Slipstitch bottom edge of jacket and lining back.

Stitch one lining sleeve to one suede sleeve on the wrist edge with right sides facing. Fold with wrong sides facing. Ease sleeve cap to fit armhole, stitching sleeve to jacket with right sides facing. Stitch jacket side seam, then the sleeve seam. Repeat for remaining side/sleeve seam.

5. To make pants, stitch outside seams of two pants with right sides facing. Then stitch inside seams with right sides facing. Repeat to make other leg. Put one leg inside the other with right sides facing. Stitch the center seam to within 1½" of waist edge (Diagram 1); backstitch. Fold waist edge ¼" to wrong side; topstitch. Sew ¼" hem on bottom edge of each leg. Sew snap set to waist at the back.

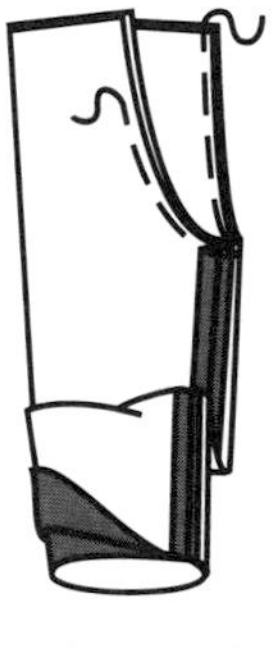

Diagram 1

6. To make cummerbund, fold each 7¼" x ⅝" satin piece, matching long edges and with wrong sides facing. On right side of design piece, baste one folded piece to each long edge, raw edges aligned. Stitch remaining satin piece to design piece, right sides facing leaving one short edge open. Turn. Zigzag opening through all layers. Sew hook and eye sets to back edges of cummerbund.

Lady Alison Cat

Stitched on blue satin using Waste Canvas 14 over 1 thread, the finished design size is 1⅞" x ⅞" for one motif. The fabric was cut 34" x 7". Begin stitching with bottom of motif 1¾" above one 34" edge. Repeat motif until stitching equals 30". Heavy lines indicate repeats. (Graph on next page.)

Step 1: Cross-stitch (2 strands)

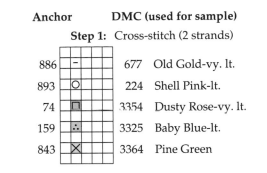

Anchor		**DMC (used for sample)**	
886	-	677	Old Gold-vy. lt.
893	O	224	Shell Pink-lt.
74	□	3354	Dusty Rose-vy. lt.
159	∴	3325	Baby Blue-lt.
843	X	3364	Pine Green

MATERIALS

Cat body and ceramic head (see Suppliers)
Completed cross-stitch design on blue satin
¾ yard of blue satin; matching thread
¾ yard of ⅜"-wide green satin ribbon
½ yard each of ⅜"-wide light blue and dark blue satin ribbons
3¾ yards of 1½"-wide blue flat lace
One ¼"-wide cameo*
Four small snap sets
One 4½"-wide mesh hat*
Five 6"-long white feathers*
Glue gun and glue
*Available at craft stores

DIRECTIONS

1. Trim design piece to 4¾" x 30¼" for skirt, with bottom of design ½" from one long edge. Cut one 15" and two 60" pieces from lace. From satin, cut the following: four jacket backs, two jacket fronts, two upper sleeves, two hat brims, two 6½" x 2¼" pieces for lower sleeves, two 3" x 1" pieces for cuffs, one 2" x 3½" piece for lower skirt, one 6" x 1½" piece for waistband and one 3"-wide circle for hat crown. Also cut 1¾"-wide bias strips, piecing as needed to equal 120".

2. To make jacket, stitch one jacket front to two jacket backs at shoulders with right sides facing. Repeat for lining. Gather 15" piece of lace to fit neck edge and baste to right side of jacket. With right sides of jacket and lining facing, match shoulder seams and stitch bottoms of back, center back, and neck edges, securing ruffle in seam. Clip curves; turn. Slipstitch bottom edge of jacket front and lining. Proceed to treat both layers of jacket as one layer.

3. To make jacket sleeve, stitch gathering threads on cap of one upper sleeve and on both long edges of one lower sleeve. Gather one edge of lower sleeve to fit straight edge of upper sleeve; stitch with right sides facing. Gather remaining edge of lower sleeve to fit cuff. Fold cuff with wrong sides facing and long raw edges aligned. Stitch cuff to lower sleeve with right sides facing. Gather the sleeve cap to fit armhole; stitch to jacket with right sides facing. Repeat for the remaining sleeve.

With right sides of jacket and sleeve facing and raw edges aligned, stitch side seam, then sleeve seam. Repeat for remaining side/sleeve seam. Sew three snap sets to center back of jacket. Center and glue cameo to jacket front (see photo).

4. To make skirt, cut bias into two 60" pieces for ruffles. Stitch a ⅛" hem on one long edge of each ruffle. Handling one ruffle and one piece of lace as one, stitch gathering threads on unhemmed edge through both layers. Repeat for remaining ruffle and lace. Gather one ruffle to fit bottom long edge of lower skirt; stitch with right sides facing. Repeat with skirt. Stitch lower skirt to skirt. Fold skirt with right sides facing and short edges aligned. Stitch to within 2" of the waist; backstitch. Press seam allowance open (including opening).

5. Fold waistband with right sides facing, matching long edges. Stitch ends (Diagram 1); turn. Stitch gathering threads on waist edge of skirt; gather to equal 5¼". Stitch waistband to waist (Diagram 2). Sew remaining snap set to back of waistband.

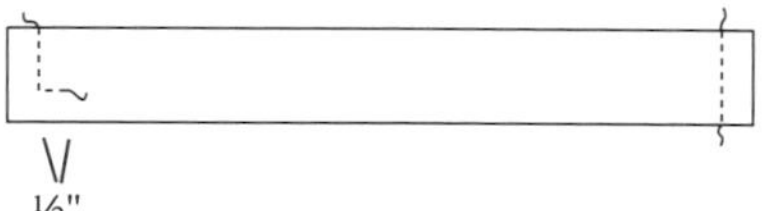

Diagram 1

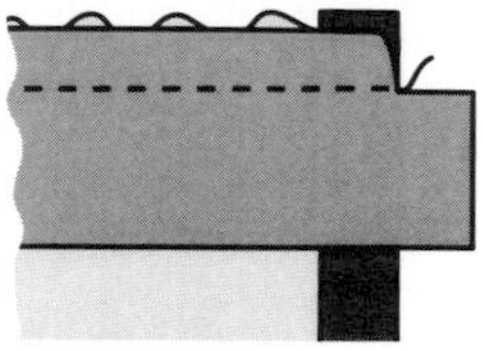

Diagram 2

6. To make hat, cut slits in one hat brim (see pattern). Stitch outside edges of brims with right sides facing. Clip curves. Turn. Fit brims over hat. Glue clipped edges inside hat, then glue top of brim to crown. Glue satin crown over hat crown.

7. To make double leaves for hat, cut six 4" lengths from green ribbon. With one length of ribbon, fold a single leaf at one end; then fold another single leaf in opposite direction at other end of ribbon (Diagram 3). Tack ribbon in center through all layers; trim excess. Repeat to make five more leaves.

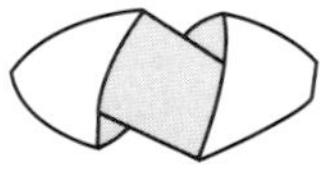

Diagram 3

To make roses for hat, cut three 4" lengths each from light and dark blue ribbons. Place one length wrong side up on a flat surface. Fold both ends of ribbon at a right angle; then hand sew gather-

Stitch Count: 26 x 12

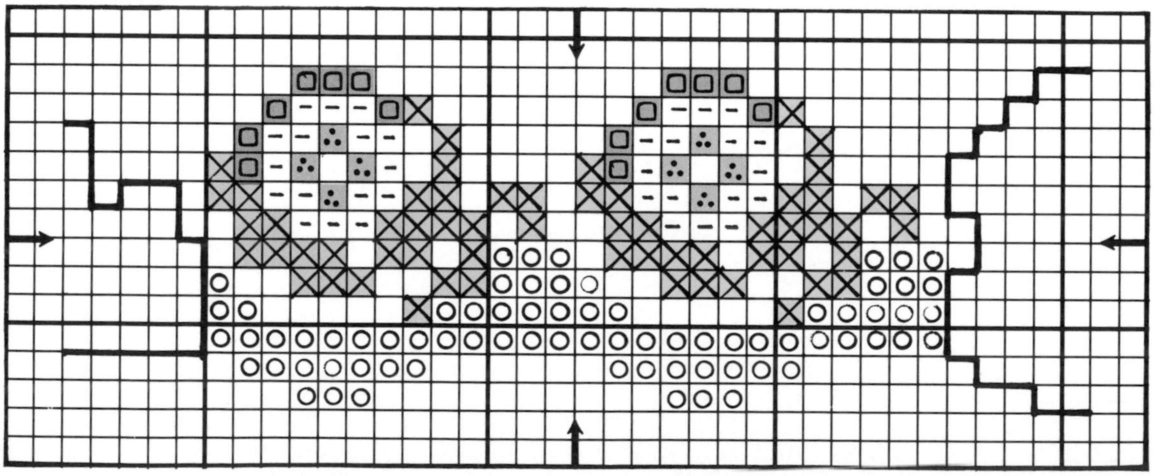

ing threads on one long edge, leaving needle and thread attached (Diagram 4).

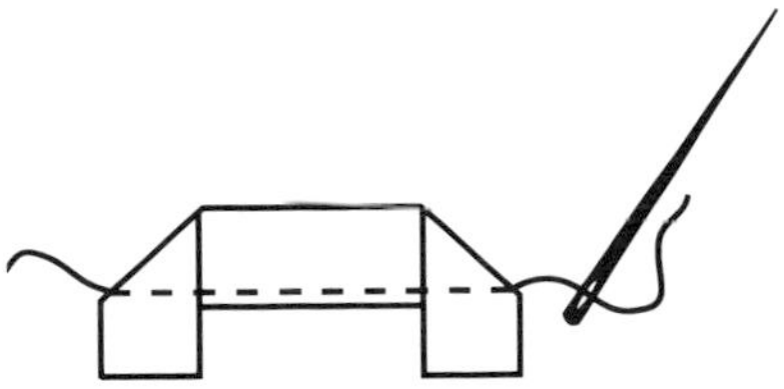

Diagram 4

Gather ribbon, wrapping in a circle, then push needle through lower edge; secure thread (Diagram 5). Trim excess ribbon. Repeat to make five more roses. Glue leaves, roses and feathers around crown as desired (see photo), placing one rose in the center of each double leaf.

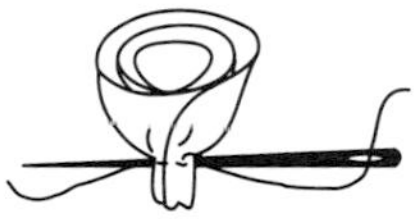

Diagram 5

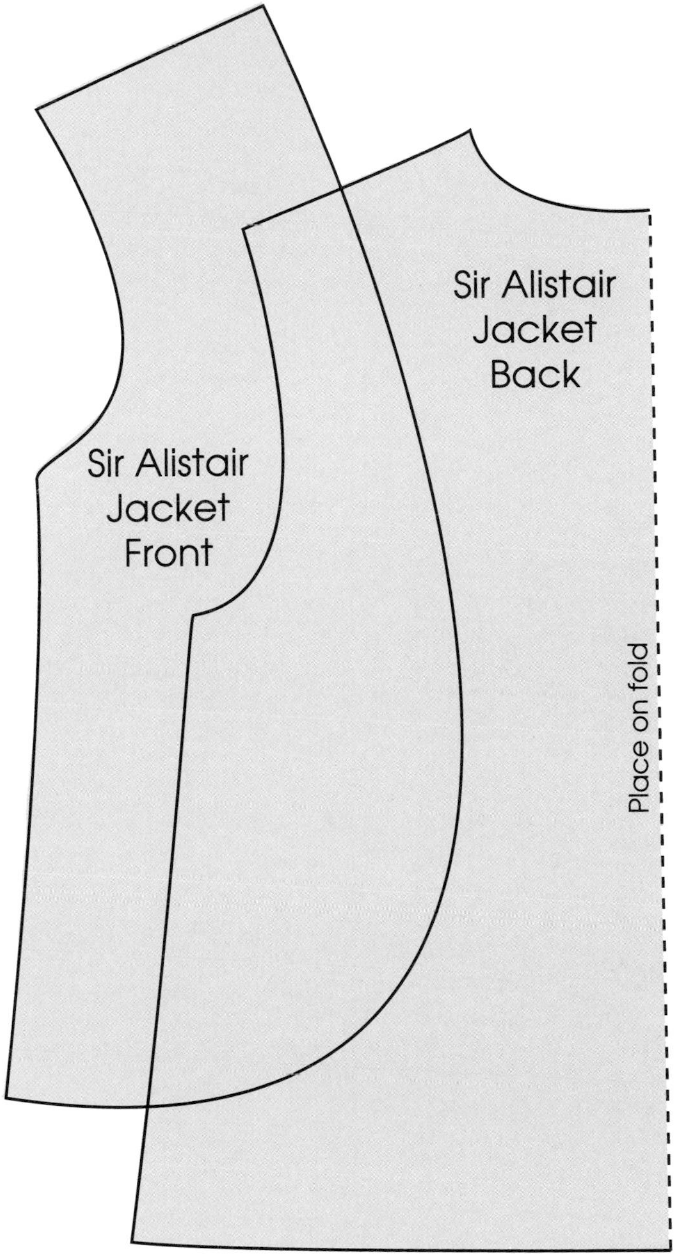

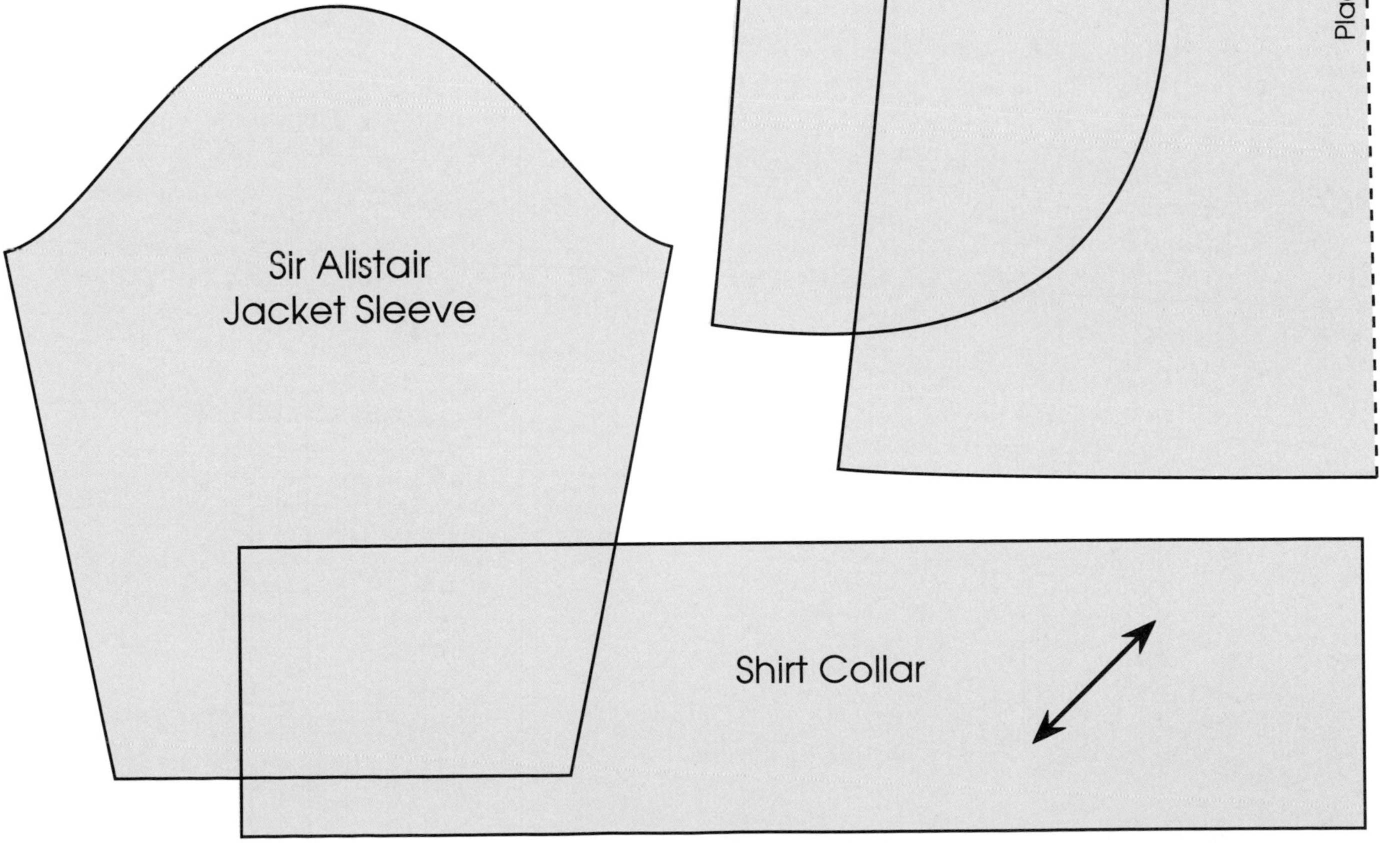

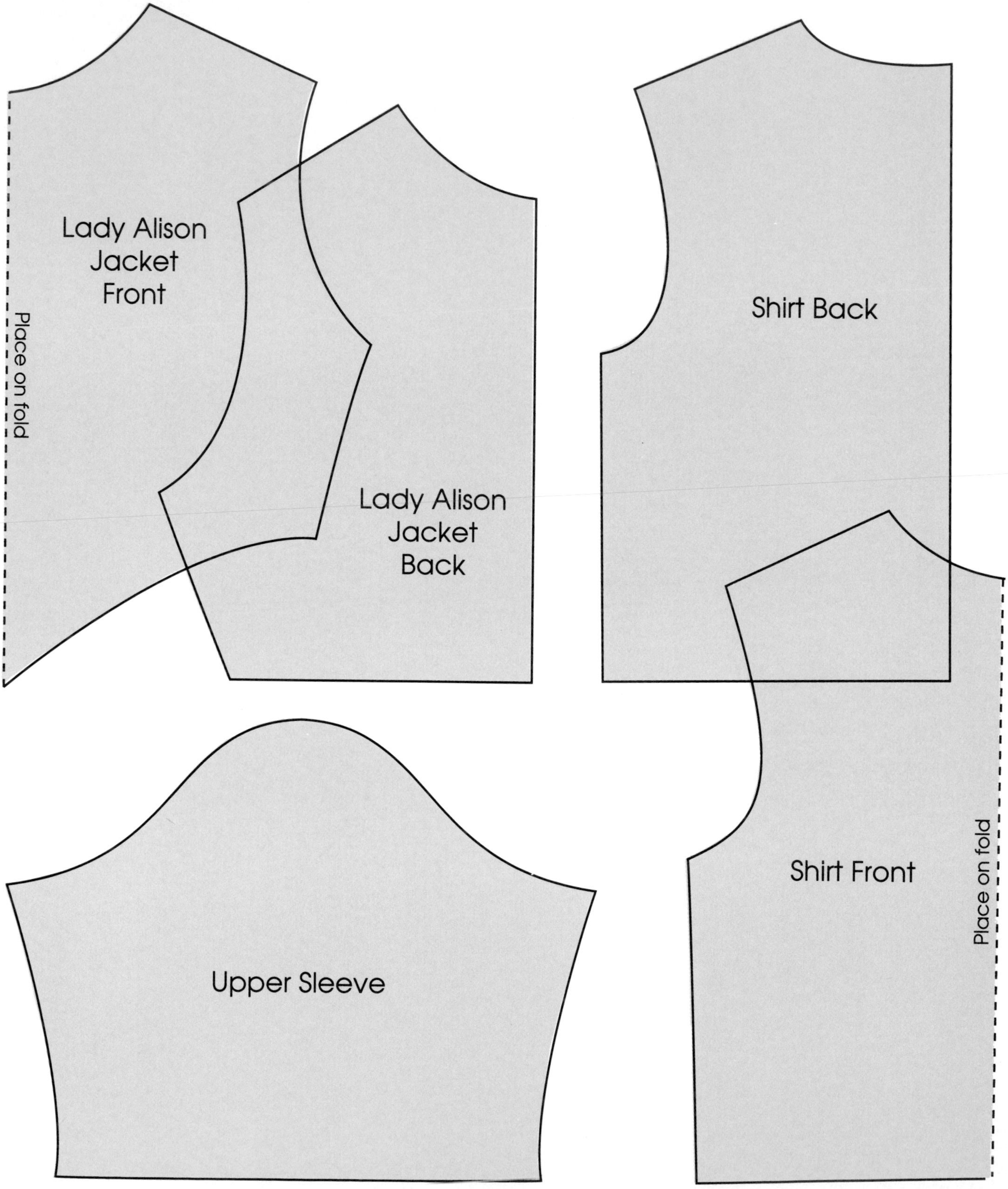
Lady Alison
Jacket
Front
Place on fold
Lady Alison
Jacket
Back
Shirt Back
Shirt Front
Place on fold
Upper Sleeve

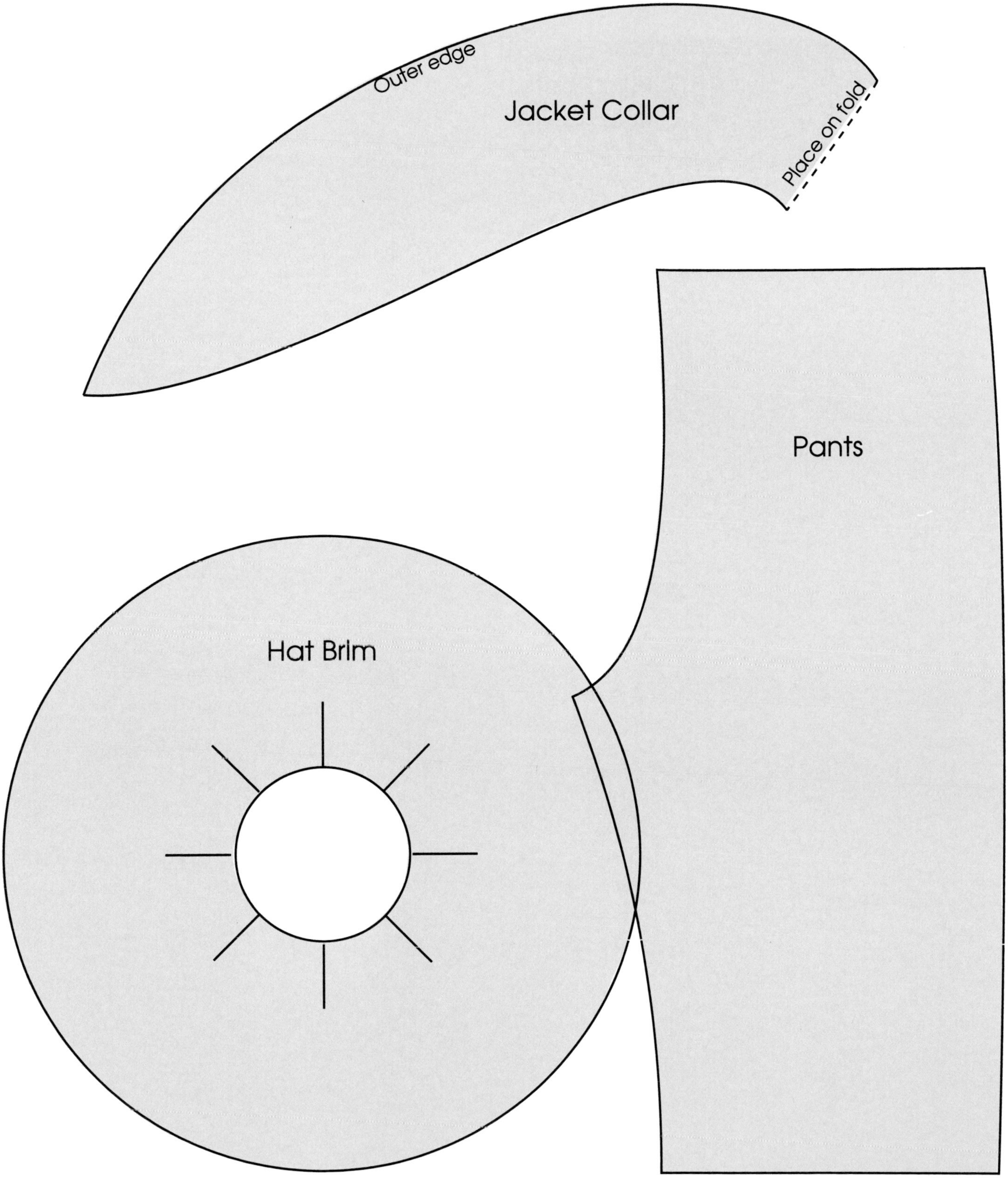
Outer edge
Jacket Collar
Place on fold
Pants
Hat Brim

In Your Easter Bonnet

Cat's collar: Stitched on pink polished cotton using Waste Canvas 14 over 1 thread, the finished design size is 1⅛" x ⅞". The fabric was cut 3" x 3".

Easter egg: Stitched on white Belfast Linen 32 over 2 threads, the finished design size is 2½" x 2½". The fabric was cut 7" x 7".

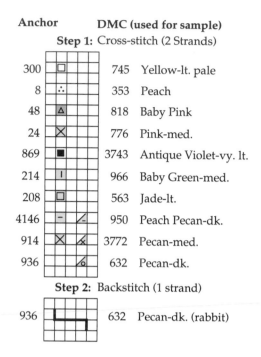

Easter Egg

Step 1: Cross-stitch (2 Strands)

Anchor	DMC (used for sample)	
300	745	Yellow-lt. pale
8	353	Peach
48	818	Baby Pink
24	776	Pink-med.
869	3743	Antique Violet-vy. lt.
214	966	Baby Green-med.
208	563	Jade-lt.
4146	950	Peach Pecan-dk.
914	3772	Pecan-med.
936	632	Pecan-dk.

Step 2: Backstitch (1 strand)

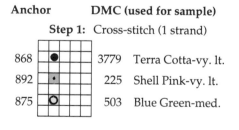

Anchor	DMC (used for sample)	
936	632	Pecan-dk. (rabbit)

Cat's Collar

Step 1: Cross-stitch (1 strand)

Anchor	DMC (used for sample)	
868	3779	Terra Cotta-vy. lt.
892	225	Shell Pink-vy. lt.
875	503	Blue Green-med.

Step 2: Backstitch (1 strand)

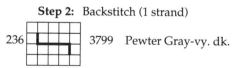

Anchor	DMC (used for sample)	
236	3799	Pewter Gray-vy. dk.

MATERIALS for cat doll
One ceramic cat head (see Suppliers)
Completed cross-stitch design on pink chintz
¼ yard of pink chintz fabric; matching thread
Scrap of white chintz; matching thread
¾ yard each of cream print, peach, sea green, and rose chintzes
One ½"-wide round pink faceted bead
One ⅜"-wide round pink faceted bead
One 16" length of ⅛"-wide pink satin ribbon
Stuffing
Buttonhole twist (matching one of above fabrics)

DIRECTIONS
1. Center collar pattern over design piece; cut one collar front. Cut one chest, four hands, two soles and four feet from white chintz. Cut one collar front, four collar backs, four ears, one bonnet back and one bonnet front from pink chintz. Cut three 7¼"-wide circles and twelve 6½"-wide circles each from pink, peach, green and cream print chintzes.

2. To make hands, stitch two hands with right sides together, leaving an opening (see pattern). Turn. Stuff firmly. Slipstitch opening closed. To shape hand, longstitch from front to back through dots (see pattern). Repeat for other hand. Set aside.

Stitch Count: 40 x 40

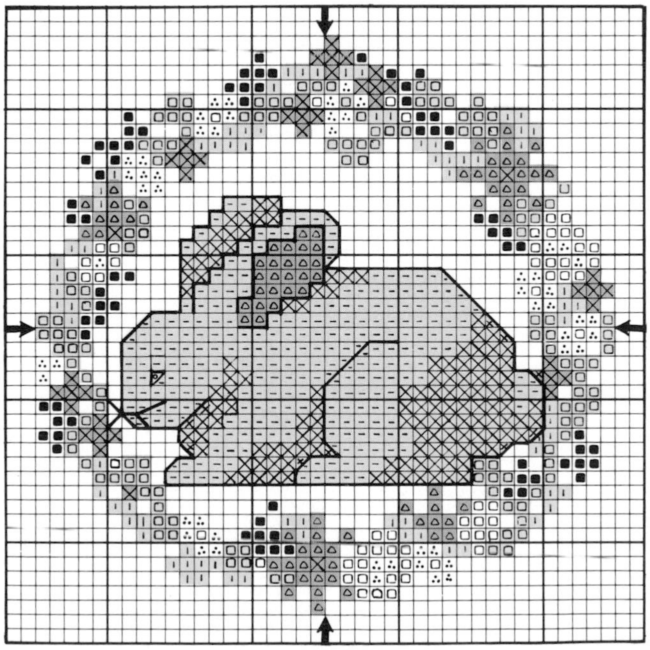

3. To make feet, stitch two feet with right sides together, leaving an opening (see pattern). Stitch sole to foot with right sides facing. Turn. Stuff firmly. Slipstitch opening closed. To shape foot, long stitch from front to back through dots (see pattern). Repeat for other foot. Set aside.

4. To make chest, stitch chest with right sides together, leaving an opening (see pattern). Turn. Stuff firmly. Slipstitch opening closed. Center and glue ceramic cat head over slipstitched edge of chest. Set aside.

5. To make finished-edge yo-yos, fold ¼" to wrong side on edges of four identical 6½" circles. Stitch gathering threads ⅛" from fold. Set aside.

To make remaining yo-yos, stitch gathering threads ¼" from raw edges of remaining circles. Gather threads tightly; knot ends of thread to secure.

6. *Note:* The smooth side of the yo-yo is the top and the gathered side is the bottom. String yo-yos with top facing bottom. The top of the last yo-yo will always face the chest once attached.

To make arm, center and whipstitch a long length of buttonhole twist at top of one hand. Then string one finished-edge yo-yo. Push yo-yo down over top of hand. Gather threads in circle tightly around hand 1½" from end of hand; secure. Next, string nine small yo-yos, alternating fabrics. Attach arm/hand securely to right side of chest. Repeat for other arm/hand; attach to left side of chest.

Stitch Count: 16 x 13

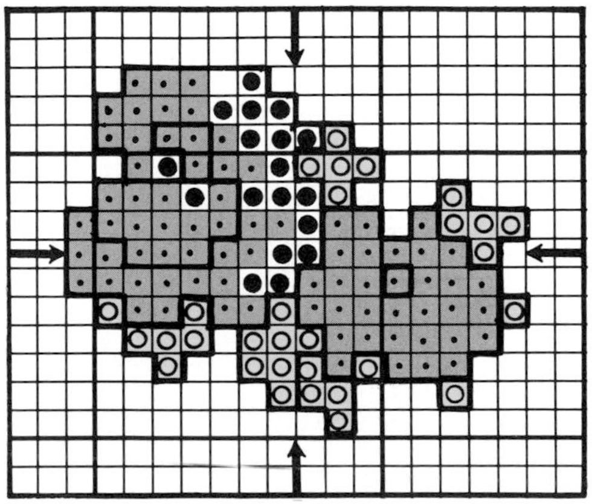

7. Repeat Step 6 above to make one leg, stringing 13 small yo-yos after foot and finished-edge yo-yo. Then thread twist with leg through one large yo-yo ½" to left of gathered center. Continue stringing large yo-yos, alternating fabrics. Next, thread needle in and out through center of chest, pulling twist tightly so yo-yos touch chest. Repeat two more times to secure; do not cut thread.

Thread needle through each large yo-yo ½" to right of gathered center. Next, string remaining small yo-yos for other leg in same sequence as first leg. Attach last finished-edge yo-yo and foot as in first leg.

8. To make collar, stitch one collar front to one collar back with right sides facing at shoulder seams; repeat. Stitch collars on outside edges with right sides facing. Turn. Slipstitch neck opening closed. Place collar on cat. Slipstitch collar together at center back. Attach beads to point on front of collar (see photo).

9. To make bonnet, fold bonnet front with right sides facing; stitch dart (Diagram 1). Repeat with back. Fold front with wrong sides together and stitch one ear to each opening through both layers (Diagram 2). Repeat with remaining ears on back. Match long edges of front, back and ears; stitch together.

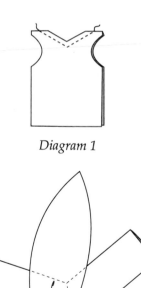

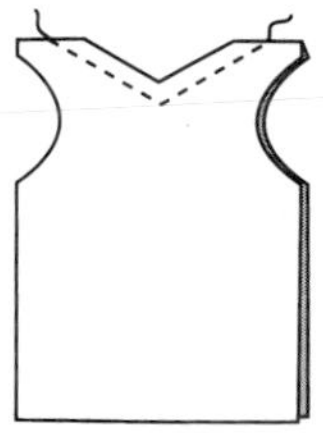

Diagram 1

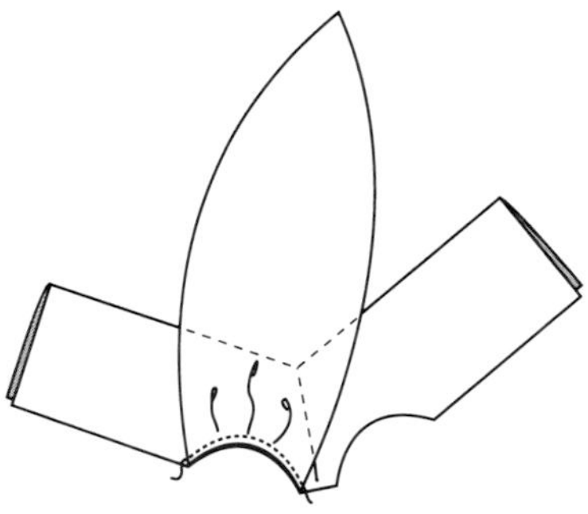

Diagram 2

10. Insert elastic between layers of back close to fold; anchor ends at raw edge. Fold raw edge to inside and topstitch. Tack back corners together. Cut ribbon in half and tack ends to front edges of bonnet.

MATERIALS for Easter egg
Completed cross-stitch design on white Belfast Linen 32; matching thread
One 6" x 7" piece of unstitched white Belfast Linen 32
2½ yards of ⅜"-wide pink satin ribbon
2½ yards of ⅛"-wide green satin ribbon
2 yards of ⅛"-wide pink satin ribbon
One 4½"-high Styrofoam egg
Paring knife
Pins
Glue

DIRECTIONS

1. Score around egg at vertical center using paring knife. Center design piece over front half of egg. Tuck into score line, taking small tucks as needed to mold fabric over the round surface. Keep the score line as narrow and inconspicuous as possible. Trim excess fabric. Place unstitched Belfast Linen over back half of egg and tuck into same score line. Trim excess fabric close to egg.

2. Cut two 18" lengths of ⅜"-wide pink ribbon and one 18" length of green ribbon. Secure one end of each piece together. Braid. Place braid over score line, beginning and ending at top of egg. Secure ends to egg with pins and/or glue.

3. Fold remaining ⅜"-wide ribbon into 3"-deep loops. Pin loops to top of egg, allowing size of each to vary. Cut one 5" length of ⅛"-wide pink ribbon. Cut remaining pink and green ribbons into 15" lengths. Tie 5" length around center of 15" lengths. Then make the 5" length into a loop to hang on the cat doll's hand. Pin and/or glue loop and 15" lengths to top of egg.

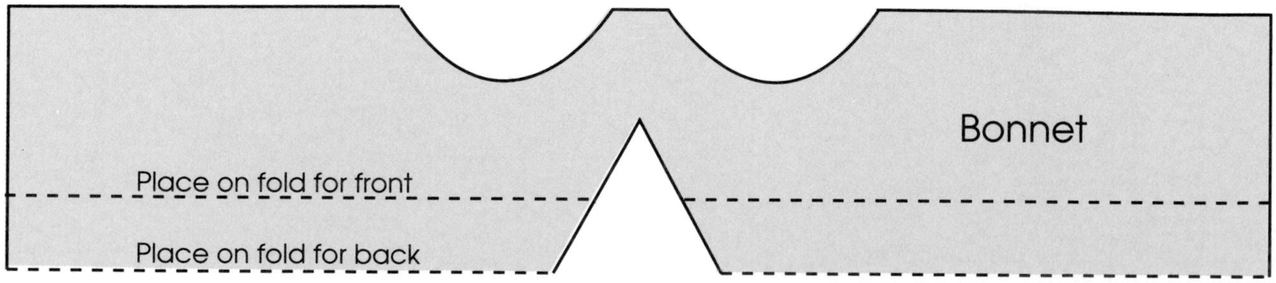

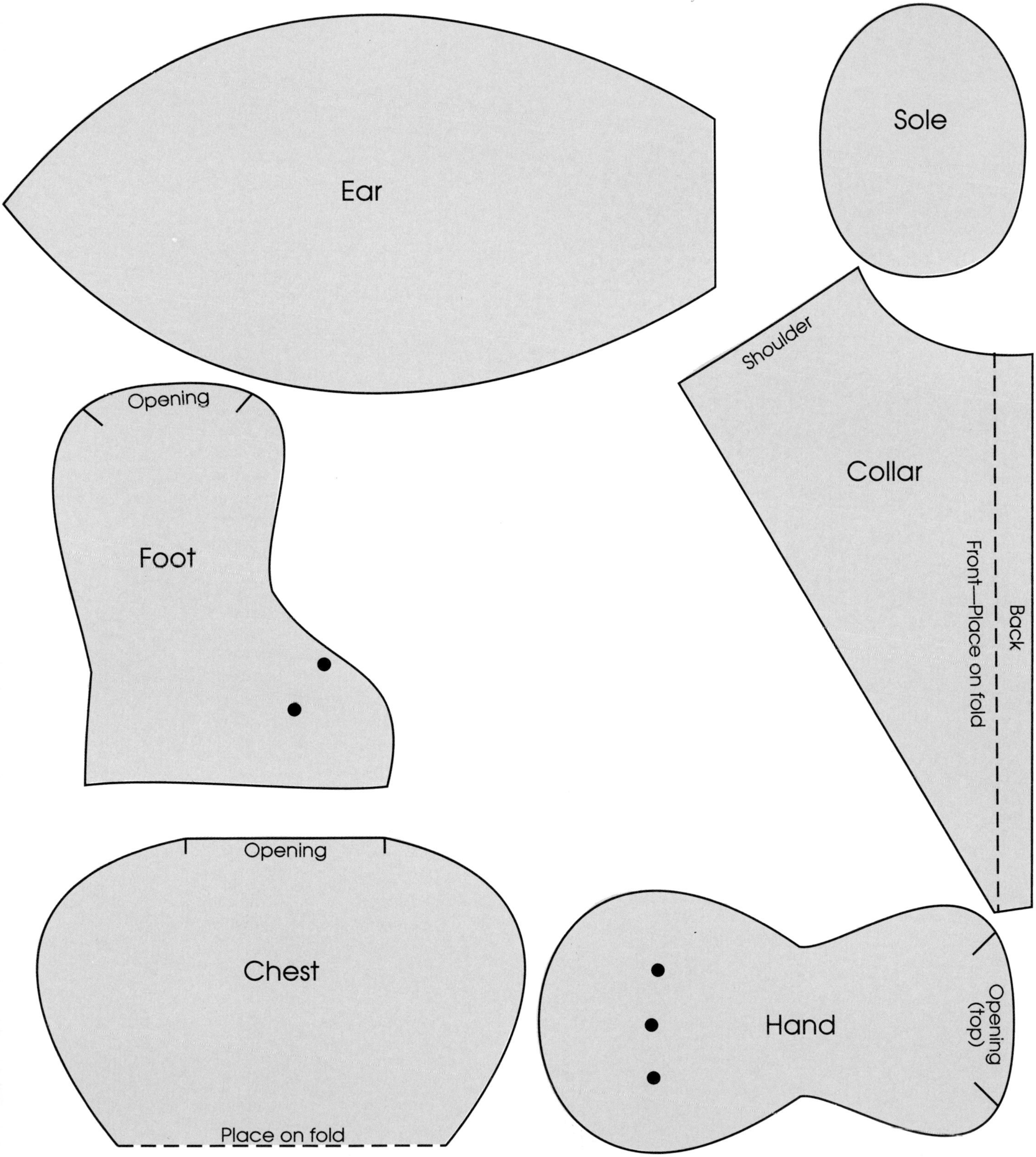
Ear
Sole
Shoulder
Collar
Front—Place on fold
Back
Opening
Foot
Opening
Chest
Place on fold
Hand
Opening (top)

Dressed for The Fourth

MATERIALS

One ceramic cat head (see Suppliers)
Scrap of cream chintz; matching thread
½ yard each of white/red stripe, white/blue print, red/white pindot, blue/white print fabrics
¾ yard of dark blue fabric; matching thread
One ⅝"-long blue faceted glass bead
One ⅜"-wide red diamond faceted glass bead
One 1-mm red glass bead
Stuffing
Buttonhole twist (matching one of above fabrics)

DIRECTIONS

1. *Note:* Patterns are on page 135. Cut one chest, four hands and four feet from cream chintz. Cut two collar fronts and four collar backs from red/white pindot. Cut 7¼"-wide circles as follows: four from white/red stripe; three from blue; and two each from white/blue print, red/white pindot, and blue/white print. Cut 6½"-wide circles as follows: eight from white/red stripe and ten each from white/blue print, red/white pindot, blue/white print and blue fabrics.

2. Complete Steps 2-7 of "In Your Easter Bonnet" (page 133).

Trick or Treat?

Stitched on cracked wheat Murano 30 over 2 threads, the finished design size is 4¼" x 2⅞". The fabric was cut 10" x 10". Begin stitching bottom of cat 3" above one edge of fabric. (Graph on page 138.)

Step 1: Cross-stitch (2 strands)

Anchor	Symbol	DMC (used for sample)	
323	•	722	Orange Spice-lt.
326	□	720	Orange Spice-dk.
75	X	3733	Dusty Rose-lt.
242	O	989	Forest Green
246	X	986	Forest Green-vy. dk.
236	O	3799	Pewter Gray-vy. dk.

Step 2: Backstitch (1 strand)

Anchor	DMC	
403	310	Black

Step 3: Satin stitch (1 strand)

Anchor	DMC	
1		White
403	310	Black

Step 4: Long stitch (2 strands)

Anchor	DMC	
403	310	Black (whiskers and inside pumpkins)

MATERIALS for doll

One ceramic cat head (see Suppliers)
Scrap of black chintz; matching thread
¾ yard each of orange/white pindot, orange/black print, light grey print, dark grey print fabrics; matching threads
One ⅜"-wide antiqued ball bead
One ½"-long antique bead
One ⅛"-wide black glass ball bead
Stuffing
Buttonhole twist (matching one of above fabrics)

DIRECTIONS

1. *Note:* Patterns are on page 135. Cut one chest, four hands, two soles and four feet from black chintz. Cut two collar fronts and four collar backs from orange/black print fabric. Cut 7½"-wide circles as follows: two from orange/black print and three each from orange/white pindot, light grey print and dark print fabrics. Cut twelve 6½"-wide circles each from orange/white pindot, orange/black print, light grey print, and dark grey print fabrics.

2. Complete Steps 2-7 of "In Your Easter Bonnet" (page 133).

MATERIALS for treat bag

Completed cross-stitch on cracked wheat Murano 30; matching thread
Scrap of unstitched cracked wheat Murano 30
¼ yard of orange/black print fabric; matching thread

DIRECTIONS

1. Trim design piece to 8" x 8" with bottom of design 2¾" above bottom edge. Cut one 8" x 8" piece and one 1" x 10" piece from unstitched Murano. Cut two 8" x 8" pieces from print fabric for lining and one 1¾" x 10" piece for handle lining.

2. Stitch side and bottom edges of design piece and unstitched 8" x 8" Murano piece together with right sides facing. Fold with side seam and bottom seam aligned and stitch 1" from corner (Diagram 1). Repeat for opposite corner. Turn. Repeat with 8" x 8" print fabric pieces. Do not turn.

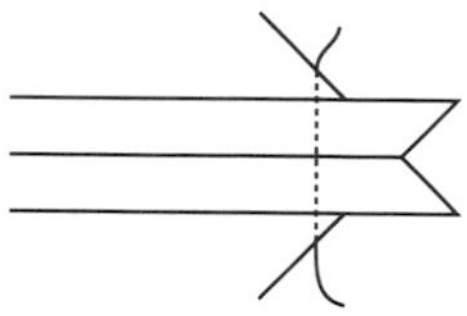

Diagram 1

3. To make handle, stitch 10" Murano piece to 10" print fabric piece on long edges with right sides facing; turn. Press with Murano at center front. Center and pin raw ends of handle over side seams of bag (Diagram 2). Slide lining over design piece with right sides facing and matching side seams. Stitch around the top edge, leaving an opening. Turn. Slipstitch opening closed. Fold lining inside bag.

Stitch Count: 64 x 43

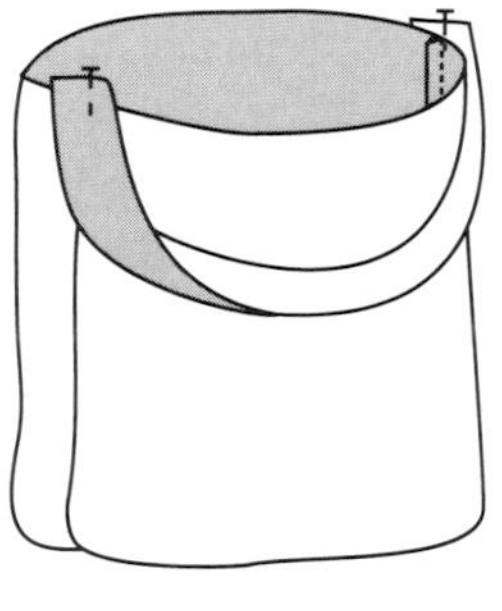

Diagram 2

Kris Kitty

The motif is from "Tiny Trimmings." Stitched on tea Linen 28 over 2 threads, the finished design size is 2¼" x 2⅛". The stitch count is 33 x 30. The fabric was cut 10" x 15". Begin stitching bottom of Christmas present 4¾" from one 10" edge and centered horizontally.

MATERIALS for cat doll
One ceramic cat head (see Suppliers)
Scrap of cream chintz; matching thread
¾ yard each of cream print and dark green fabrics
½ yard each of burgundy, dark green print, dark green/burgundy stripe fabrics
Two ½"-wide dark green round faceted beads
One ⅜"-wide burgundy round faceted bead
One ⅜"-wide dark green round faceted bead
One ¼"-wide burgundy round faceted bead
One green seed bead
Stuffing
Buttonhole twist (matching one of above fabrics)

DIRECTIONS
1. Cut one chest, four hands, two soles and four feet from cream chintz. Cut two collar fronts and four collar backs from dark green fabric. Cut one hat from burgundy fabric. Cut one 6½" x 2" dark green/burgundy stripe piece for hat band. Cut 7¼"-wide circles as follows: six from cream print, four from dark green and two from dark green print. Cut 6½"-wide circles as follows: eight from cream print, 12 from burgundy, 10 from dark green, 10 from dark green print and eight from dark green/burgundy stripe fabrics.

2. Complete Steps 2-7 from "In Your Easter Bonnet" (page 133).

3. To make hat, fold hat band with wrong sides facing lengthwise to measure 6½" x 1". With right sides facing and long straight edges aligned, stitch band to hat, easing fullness as you sew; fold seam allowance to wrong side of hat. With remaining straight edges aligned and right sides facing, stitch. Turn and attach one ⅜"-wide green bead, then the seed bead to point of hat. Place hat on cat.

MATERIALS for toy bag
Completed cross-stitch design on tea Linen 28 over 2 threads
One 8" x 13" piece of unstitched tea Linen 28
Scrap of cream chintz; matching thread
Scrap of fleece
¾ yard of blue rayon cord
Two ⅝"-wide brass jingle bells
One sharp large-eyed needle
Stuffing
Assorted small toys and packages

DIRECTIONS
1. Trim design piece to 8" x 13" with bottom of design 2¾" from bottom edge. Cut two 6½" x 13" pieces each from cream chintz and fleece.

2. Stitch side and bottom edges of design piece and unstitched linen with right sides facing. Fold with side and bottom seam matching and right sides facing. Stitch across seam 1" from corner (Diagram 1, page 138). Repeat for opposite corner. Turn.

3. Layer fleece on wrong side of each cream piece. Stitch side and bottom edges with right sides facing,

catching fleece in seam. Stitch corners (see Step 2). Slide lining over design piece with right sides facing and matching side seams. Stitch around top edge, leaving an opening. Trim fleece from seams. Turn. Slipstitch opening closed. Fold lining inside the bag.

4. Thread rayon cord into needle. Beginning near one side seam, sew ½"-long running stitches 2¾" below and parallel to top edge. Fill bottom of bag with stuffing. Draw up cord slightly; knot. Tie into bow. Fill top of bag with toys and packages.

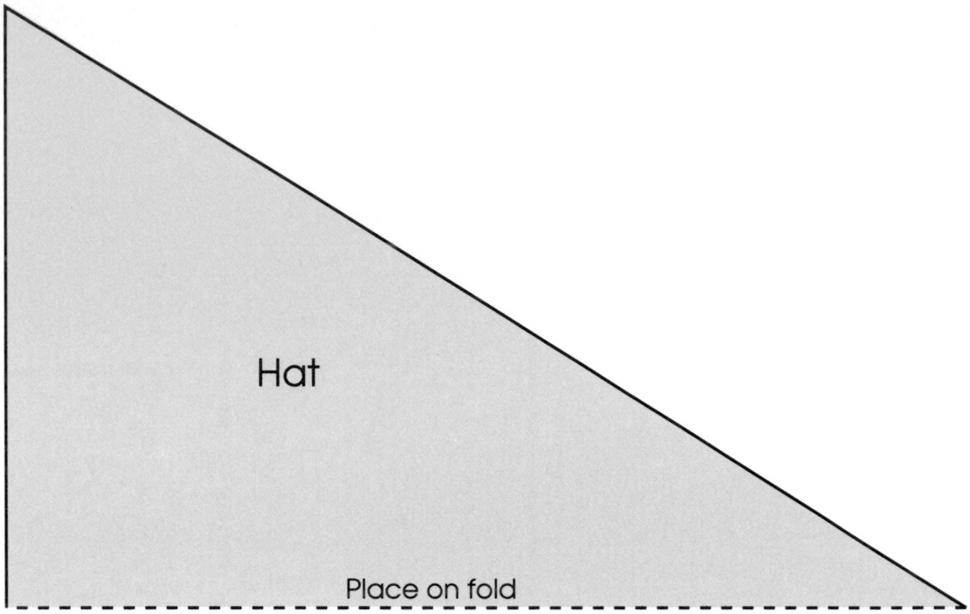

General Instructions

Backstitch: Complete all cross-stitching before working back stitches or other accent stitches. Working from left to right with one strand of floss (unless otherwise instructed in code), bring needle and thread up at A, down at B, and up again at C. Going back down at A, continue in this manner.

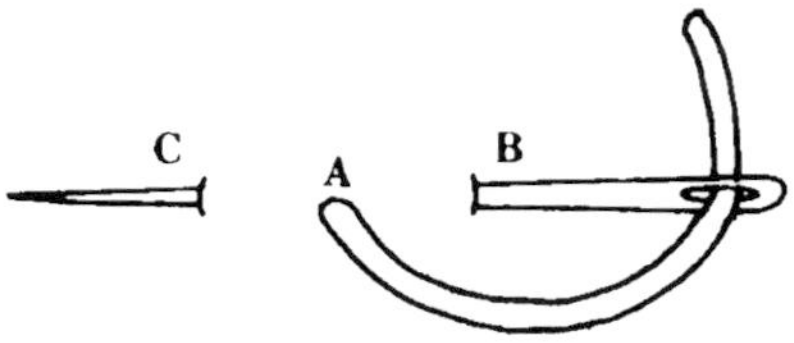

Beadwork: Attach beads to fabric with a half-cross, lower left to upper right. Secure beads before returning thread through beads, lower right to upper left. Complete row of half-crosses before returning to secure all beads.

Bias strip: Fold the fabric at a 45° angle to the grain and crease. Cut on the crease. Cut additional pieces the width indicated in the instructions and parallel to the first cutting line. The ends of the pieces should be on the grain of the fabric. Place the right sides of the ends together and stitch with a ¼" seam. Continue to connect the pieces until the bias strip equals the length indicated in the instructions.

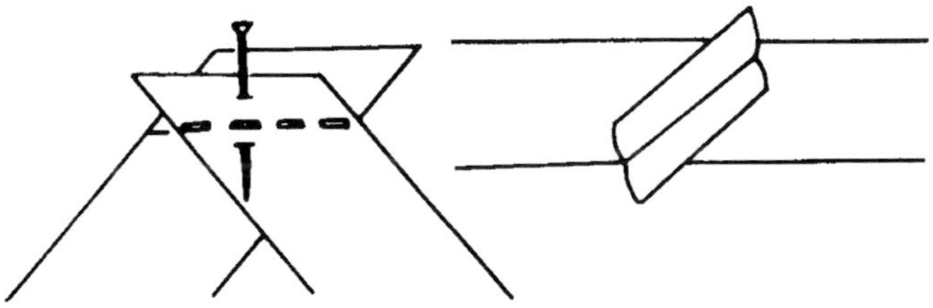

Cleaning work: Always clean your completed work when all stitching is complete. Soak the stitched piece in cold water with a mild soap for 5 to 10 minutes. Rinse and roll in a towel to remove excess water; do not wring. Place the work face down on a dry towel and, with iron on a warm setting, iron until work is dry.

Corded piping: Place the cording in the center of the wrong side of the bias strip and fold the fabric over it. Using a zipper foot, stitch close to the cording through both layers of fabric. Trim the seam allowance ¼" from the stitching line.

Corded tubing: Fold the bias over the cording with right sides facing and raw edges aligned. Fold cording in half; mark the center on the fold. Place one end of the bias ¼" beyond the center of the cording. Using a zipper foot, stitch ¼" from the center of the cording on the bias strip. Then stretch the bias slightly while stitching the long edge close to the cording. Trim the seam allowance. Turn, slowly drawing the enclosed cord out of the tubing; the free cord will be pulled into the tubing automatically. Trim the stitched end and excess cording.

Cross-stitch: For a smooth cross-stitch, use the "push and pull" method. Push the needle straight down and completely through fabric before pulling. Do not pull the thread tightly. The tension should be consistent throughout, making the stitches even. Make one cross for each symbol on the chart. Bring needle and thread up at A, down at B, up at C, and down again at D.

For rows, stitch from left to right, then back. All stitches should lie in the same direction.

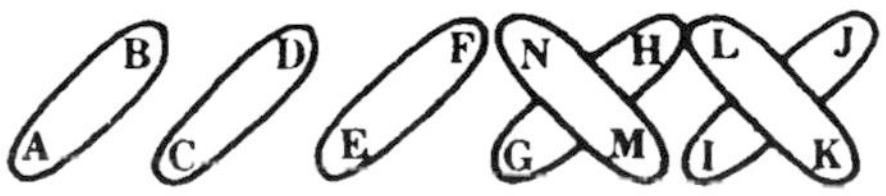

Fabric: To select fabric, refer to the project's sample paragraph. Counted cross-stitch is usually worked on even-weave fabric. These fabrics are manufactured specifically for counted thread embroidery and are woven with the same number of vertical as horizontal threads per inch. Because the number of threads in the fabric is equal in each direction, each stitch will be the same size. It is the number of threads per inch in even-weave fabric that determines the size of a finished design.

To prepare the even-weave fabric, cut it at least 3" larger on all sides than the design size, or cut it the size specified in the sample paragraph. A 3" margin is the minimum amount of space that allows for working the edges of the design comfortably. If the item is to be finished into a sachet bag, for example, the fabric should be cut as directed. To keep fabric from fraying, whipstitch or machine zigzag the raw edges.

When the instructions call for a fabric such as cotton or chintz, keep in mind that all measurements in the instructions are based on a 45"-wide piece.

Always use a dressmakers' pen or chalk to mark on fabric. It will wash out when you clean your finished piece.

Floss: To select floss, refer to the project's code—all numbers and color names are cross referenced between ANCHOR and DMC brands of floss. Run the floss over a damp sponge to straighten. Use lengths no longer than 18". Separate all six strands and use the number of strands called for in the code. If floss becomes twisted, drop the needle and allow the floss to unwind itself.

To secure floss on fabric, start by inserting needle up from the underside of the fabric at starting point. Hold 1" of floss behind the fabric and stitch over it, securing the first few stitches. To finish floss, run under four or more stitches on the back of the design. Never knot floss unless working on clothing.

Another method for securing floss is the waste knot. Knot floss and insert needle from the right side of the fabric about 1" from the design area. Work several stitches over the floss to secure. Cut off the knot later.

To carry floss, weave floss under the previously worked stitches on the back. Do not carry the floss across any fabric that is not or will not be stitched. Loose threads, especially dark ones, will show through the fabric.

French Knot: Bring the needle up at A, using one strand of embroidery floss. Wrap floss around needle two times (unless other instructed in directions). Insert needle beside A, pulling floss until it fits snugly around needle. Pull needle through to back.

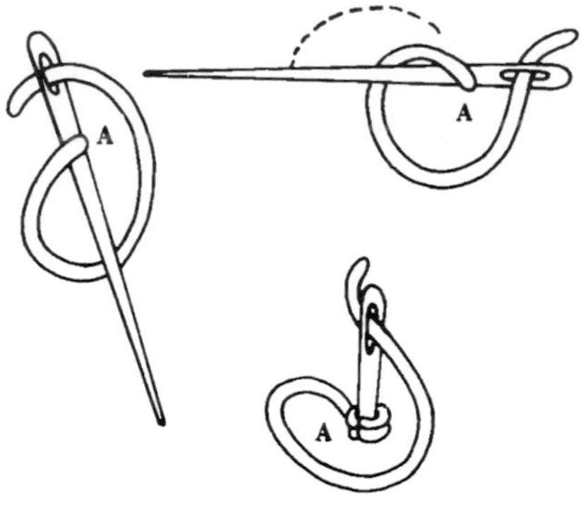

Gathers: Machine-stitch two parallel rows of long stitches ¼" and ½" from the edge of the fabric (unless otherwise instructed in directions). Leave the ends of the thread 2" or 3" long. Pull the two bobbin threads and gather to fit the desired length. Long edges may need to be gathered from both ends. Disperse the fullness evenly and secure the threads in the area by wrapping them around a pin in a figure eight.

Graph: Locate the center of the design on the graph by following the vertical and horizontal arrows.

When a graph spans more than one page, the bottom two rows of the graph on the previous page are repeated, separated by a small space, indicating where to connect them.

Hem: Turn edges double ⅛" to equal ¼", unless otherwise instructed in directions.

Pattern: Trace all patterns using tracing paper. All patterns include a ¼" seam allowance unless otherwise specified.

Some full-size patterns are too large to include on a page; therefore, they are reduced and transferred to a grid. Each square of the grid equals 1". To enlarge these patterns, mark grid lines on a large sheet of paper, 1" apart, to fill the paper. Begin marking dots on 1" grid lines where the reduced pattern intersects the corresponding grid line. Connect the dots.

Potpourri: Follow the recipes below to make the potpourri for a specific project. Because potpourri recipes are adaptable to the availability of ingredients, remember your likes and dislikes when substituting. Powders and spices serve as fixatives for aromas so they won't dissipate overnight. Use open-weave and natural fiber fabrics to encase potpourris and sachets in pouches. Synthetic fabrics, which are more tightly woven, are more resistant to odors.

Strawberry Sachet (Country Coziness)
6 ounces dried chopped strawberries
3 ounces dried rose petals
1½ tablespoons salt
3 ounces unscented talcum powder
12 ounces cornstarch

Flower and Spice (Gloriously Scented Goose)
1 pint rose petals (may add petals of other fragrant flowers)
¾ cup pure salt
Grated rind of ½ orange or lemon
1 teaspoon ground cinnamon
1 teaspoon ground cloves

Carnation Potpourri (The Scents of Fall)
1 pint carnations
½ pint chrysanthemums (to add color and bulk to the mixture)
1 teaspoon cloves
1 tablespoon salt
1 ounce benzoin gum powder (available at craft stores)

Running stitch: Bring needle in and out in loose ¼" intervals, leaving tails long enough to gather materials. A running stitch is usually used to gather finished edges, such as a neckline or a wrist.

Satin stitch: Make parallel stitches to fill in area. Stitches can be worked vertically or diagonally. Follow the direction of the symbol on the graph.

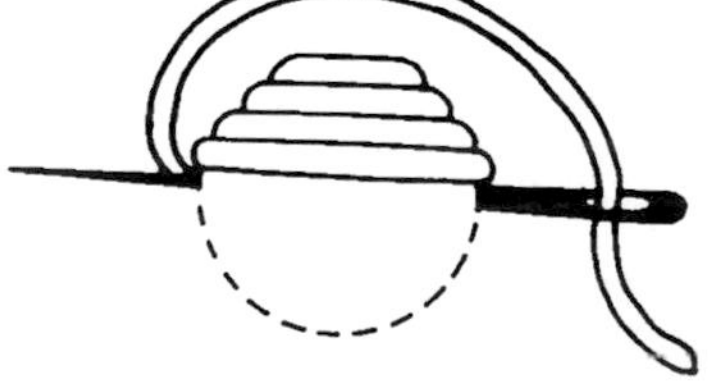

Seam allowance: Always use ¼" seam allowances unless otherwise specified in the instructions.

Slipstitch: Insert needle at A, slide it through the folded edge of the fabric for about ⅛" to ¼" and bring it out at B. Directly below B, take a small stitch through the second piece of fabric.

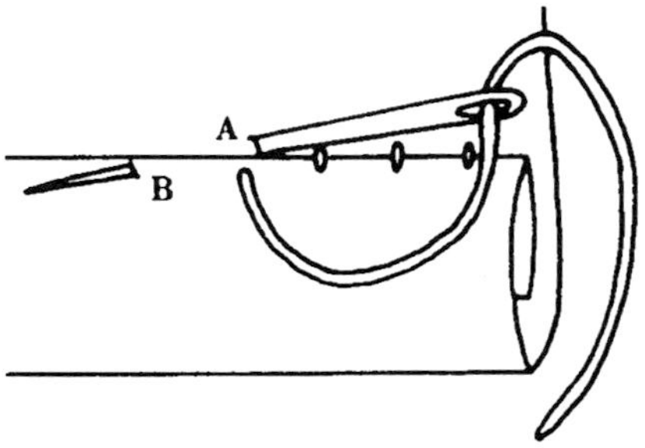

Waste Canvas: Cut the waste canvas 1" larger on all sides than the finished design size. Baste the waste canvas to the fabric to be stitched. Complete the stitching. Then, dampen the stitched area with cold water. Pull the waste canvas threads out one at a time with tweezers. It is easier to pull all the threads running in one direction first, then pull out the remaining threads. Allow the stitching to dry. Place design piece face down on a towel and iron.

Yarn ringlet hair: Wrap damp acrylic yarn around coat hanger and put in warm oven, 200°-250°, for about 10 minutes; check frequently. Allow to cool. Remove acrylic yarn from hanger; use as directed.

Suppliers

All products are available retail from Shepherd's Bush, 220 24th Street, Ogden, UT 84401; 801-399-4546. Or, for a merchant near you, write to the following suppliers:

Acadia Yarn
Classic Elite Yarns, 12 Perkins St., Lowell, MA 01854

Aida 14 (cream, ivory); **Belfast Linen** 32 (cream, driftwood, white); **Damask Aida 14** (cream); **Dublin Linen 25** (mocha, pink); **Hardanger 22** (beige); **Jobelan 28** (white); **Linda 27** (khaki); **Murano 30** (amaretto, cracked wheat, pewter); **Pastel Linen 28** (cream); **Waste Canvas 14**
Joan Toggit Ltd., 35 Fairfield Place, West Caldwell, NJ 07006

Filatura Di Crosa Sympathie Yarn
Stacie Charles Collection, 117 Dobbins St., Brooklyn, NY 11222

Linen 28 (tea)
Charles Craft, P.O. Box 1049, Perkins St., Lowell, MA 01854

Paternayan Persian Yarn
Johnson Creative Arts, P.O. Box 158, 445 Main St., West Townsend, MA 01474

Pebble Beads
Gay Bowles Sales, Inc., 1310 Plainfield Avenue, P.O. Box 1060, Janesville, WI 53547

Porcelain Cat
Vanessa-Ann Afghan Weave 18
Chapelle Designers, Box 9252 Newgate Station, Ogden, UT 84409

Silk ribbons
Y.L.I. Corp., P.O. Box 109 (mail orders), 482 Freedom Blvd. (inquiries), Provo, UT 84603 and 84601, respectively

Index

All of us at Meredith® Press are dedicated to offering you, our customer, the best books we can create. We are particularly concerned that all of the instructions for making projects are clear and accurate. Please address your correspondence to Customer Service Department, Meredith® Press, Meredith Corporation, 150 East 52nd Street, New York, NY 10022.

The Changing Seasons: An American Sampler is the fourth in a series of cross-stitch books. If you would like the first three books in the series, *Quilt Designs in Cross-Stitch: An America Sampler 1989, Country Cross-Stitch Designs: An American Sampler 1990,* and *Home Is Where the Heart Is: An American Sampler*, please write to Better Homes and Gardens Books, P.O. Box 10670, Des Moines, IA 50336, or call 1-800-678-2665.